Governance of Land Use in Poland

THE CASE OF ŁÓDŹ

Please cite this publication as:
OECD (2016), *Governance of Land Use in Poland: The Case of Łódź*, OECD Publishing, Paris.
http://dx.doi.org/10.1787/9789264260597-en

ISBN 978-92-64-26053-5 (print)
ISBN 978-92-64-26059-7 (PDF)

The statistical data for Israel are supplied by and under the responsibility of the relevant Israeli authorities. The use of such data by the OECD is without prejudice to the status of the Golan Heights, East Jerusalem and Israeli settlements in the West Bank under the terms of international law.

Latvia was not an OECD member at the time of preparation of this publication. Accordingly, Latvia is not included in the area totals.

Photo credits: Cover illustration: © Jeffrey Fisher.

Corrigenda to OECD publications may be found on line at: *www.oecd.org/about/publishing/corrigenda.htm.*

Foreword

How land is used affects a wide range of factors – from day-to-day quality of life factors such as the availability of food and clean water and the length of daily commutes, to the long-term sustainability of urban and rural communities, including the possibility for climate change adaptation and mitigation. How governments regulate land use and address public and private investment, how competencies are allocated across levels of government, and how land use is taxed, is critical.

Like many OECD countries, Poland has a nested system of spatial planning, but local governments are the main actors in land-use planning. They have responsibility for creating and approving local spatial development plans, which are the only legally binding zoning plans in Poland. The national government sets the framework law and provides guidance for lower order plans. Regional governments elaborate regional spatial plans, which outline major regional development and investment priorities.

While the governance of land use in Poland is evolving in promising directions, there is still scope for reform. A major issue is that while municipalities elaborate planning documents to guide future developments, planning coverage remains low in many cases and such documents are thus ineffective. This report focuses on the city of Łódź and its peri-urban areas. This city was chosen because of the major opportunities and challenges it faces. Planned urban regeneration and recent transportation infrastructure developments increase the attractiveness of the city for residents, businesses and investors. However, uncontrolled sprawl, together with a shrinking population, threaten the future sustainability of the city in fiscal, economic, environmental and social terms. Effective land-use planning will be critical to Łódź's future success, including its aim of developing as a more compact city.

The importance of better understanding land-use policies has been underscored by a wide range of developments, including the recent formation and subsequent bursting of real-estate bubbles in a number of OECD countries, the growth of renewable energy production, changing demographics, the provision of public services including public transport, environmental concerns, spatial planning, changes in lifestyles, tourism and growing food security concerns. These examples illustrate the strong relationship that exists between land-use policies, social development, and macroeconomic trends and fluctuations across both urban and rural territories.

The interactions between institutions and markets can heavily influence the supply, availability, function and location of land. A major function of the planning system is to balance property rights against the public interest by translating spatial development processes into physical form. Land-use regulations and tax regimes create various incentives and disincentives that are played out across landscapes. The interface between these issues is complex and often contested, in particular on the fringes of urban and rural areas, in brownfield redevelopment zones, and in areas of social deprivation. Any policy interventions therefore need to be carefully designed to be effective. A major role of planning is to proactively address and mediate these conflicts where they occur. This requires strong public engagement and communication, hence a growing tradition of collaborative and communicative planning. Given the "nestedess" of spatial planning, it is no surprise that determining the appropriate level of planning, regulation oversight and implementation is difficult. Moreover, forms of land governance depend on the institutional history of a country and are often influenced by the country-specific evolution of the system of property rights and land-use planning.

In recognition of the importance of these issues, the OECD's Regional Development Policy Committee (RDPC) and its Working Party on Urban Policy (WPURB) and the Working Party on Rural Policy (WPRUR) have undertaken a programme of research on the governance of land use. This case study of spatial and land-use planning in Poland is the first of several case studies that will be published together with an inventory and analysis of land-use planning systems across all OECD countries.

Acknowledgements

The OECD *Governance of Land Use in Poland: The Case of Łódź* contributes to a larger multi-country study of land use in select OECD countries being produced by the OECD Public Governance and Territorial Development Division led by Rolf Alter and its Regional Development Policy Division under the leadership of Joaquim Oliveira Martins. This report was made possible through the support of the government of Poland and specifically, the Ministry of Economic Development.

This report was co-ordinated by Tamara Krawchenko, under the supervision of Rudiger Ahrend and Jose Enrique Garcilazo. It was drafted by Tamara Krawchenko with input from Abel Schumann, OECD Secretariat, and David Freshwater, University of Kentucky.

The OECD Secretariat wishes to extend warm thanks to the exceptional team of officials responsible for the day-to-day management of this project in Poland: Monika Andrzejewska, Wojciech Wroblewski and Anna Komorowska of the Polish Ministry of Economic Development. They brought together a wide variety of perspectives to inform the report and we are most grateful for their management, expertise and guidance.

The Secretariat is also grateful for the co-operation and support of the numerous officials, experts and private sector representatives in Łódź who shared their insights with the team preparing for the review and in other ways participated in the study. The Secretariat extends a special thank you to Bartosz Poniatowski, Branch Manager of Landscape and Aesthetics of the City of Łódź and Lukasz Pancewicz, Chief Urban Planner, Łódź Municipal Planning Bureau. We would also like to thank officials in the rural municipality of Nowosolna for their contributions to the study.

This report benefited from the peer review of Dr. Jaromír Hainc of the Prague Institute of Planning and Development. The Secretariat thanks him for his insights and for attending the Mission and sharing his knowledge with the local team. We would also like to extend thanks to Adam Ostry, Governance Reviews and Partnerships Division, for supporting the initial stages of this project. Finally, many thanks to Justine Boulant for producing several of the maps, and to Pilar Philip for preparing the report for publication (both of the Regional Development Policy Division).

Table of contents

Tables

Figures

Boxes

Acronyms and abbreviations

GDP	Gross domestic product
INSPIRE	Infrastructure for Spatial Information in the European Community
ITI	European Union integrated territorial investments
NCL	New Centre of Łódź
NGO	Non-governmental organisation
NSDC	National Spatial Development Concept
PLN	Polish zloty
ROP	Regional operational programmes
SCoT	Territorial Coherence Plan (France) *Schéma de cohérence territoriale*
SEZ	Special economic zones

Executive summary

Key findings

This case study of the governance of land use in Łódź illustrates many promising practices and offers guidance on how to make the governance structure and planning system more coherent and robust both in Łódź and in Poland more generally. Łódź, the third-largest city in Poland, is presently undertaking several major projects that have the potential to significantly reinvigorate the economy after a period of economic decline following the collapse of its traditional manufacturing industries in the late 1990s. A raft of infrastructure investments and new developments are transforming its city centre and increasing its transportation connectivity. Coherent land-use practices across the areas where people live and work will be critical in order for the city and its surrounding communities to develop in a socially, environmentally and fiscally sustainable way.

Uncontrolled sprawl is undermining the city's future development

The city's population is declining and is projected to shrink dramatically over the next few decades while new developments continue apace in suburban and peri-urban areas. These patterns of uncontrolled sprawl pose a real challenge for Łódź's fiscal and environmental sustainability, as well as its potential agglomeration benefits. This has cost implications as the city will need to maintain services and infrastructure in established areas. The city seeks a more compact and sustainable urban form with a vibrant city centre, but the various tools at its disposal are not meeting this goal. Current fiscal and regulatory tools do not adequately address uncontrolled sprawl. Local spatial development plans only cover 10% of the city's territory at present due to long delays in adopting new plans. Consequently, short-term one-off planning decisions are made for areas not included in the plans.

Parallel and disconnected measures in the planning system limit its effectiveness

Certain elements of the Polish planning system are inconsistent, leading to suboptimal outcomes. These include: 1) the special infrastructural acts of the national government, which suspend local planning law and are overused; 2) areas without local spatial development plans which are subject to one-off planning decisions; and 3) special economic zones (SEZ), which are not linked to local spatial objectives. These mechanisms undermine coherent and consistent planning at the local level.

An integrated approach is needed for planning and development

Poland's national spatial policy recognises the importance of planning based on functional urban areas – that is, the area in which people live, work and commute. But in Łódź, collaboration among urban, peri-urban and rural locales is only just beginning. Although recent measures and legislation encourage such collaborative action (e.g. the European Union's integrated territorial investments [ITIs], the 2015 Metropolitan Association Act and the 2015 Revitalisation Act), Poland needs to ensure that such initiatives can be sustained over time. This entails finding the right geographic scale to work on issues and the corresponding appropriate institutional structures for co-operation.

Policy recommendations

To address the three main challenges noted above, this report makes the following recommendations:

- Enhance incentives and governance structures for municipalities to undertake planning based on the functional urban areas. Although the EU's ITIs require municipalities to form association agreements in order to undertake joint projects, the national government should consider ways to support these nascent associations through dedicated funding streams and/or regulatory measures such as common spatial plans.
- Strengthen the links among spatial, economic and sectoral plans at the local level both within and among municipalities. Joint indicators that assess and monitor actions over time can help to achieve this. The new Revitalisation Act (2015) is a promising first step to better integrating spatial and sectoral plans in targeted areas. More should be done to encourage such approaches.
- Łódź should expand the coverage of its local spatial development plans to meet its objective of a more compact urban form. Reliance on the planning decision mechanism should be reduced in the short term, and eliminated in the longer term. Reliance on special infrastructural acts should be reduced and, in the longer term eliminated, and developments should proceed through the regular planning system.
- To manage spatial issues more effectively, municipalities should employ a broader range of tools, particularly fiscal ones. The new Revitalisation Act (2015) allows a municipality to use an adjacency levy and expanded real estate tax in designated areas in order to better capture increase in land value resulting from public investments.
- The compensation paid to owners if they are negatively affected by a local spatial development plan inhibits the adoption of new plans, which are sorely needed. Some limits should be introduced to mitigate this effect, such as reducing the timeframe in which owners can apply for compensation, which is currently unlimited. Further, the way that the property tax is calculated (based on land and building size/area) is inefficient and can encourage land speculation. Local governments are not reaping the benefits of a rise in land values when local infrastructure investments are made. A shift to *ad valorum* property taxation is warranted to capture these changes in value.

- The links between spatial planning and demographic, socio-economic, and fiscal analysis and forecasting should be strengthened. Indicators related to spatial development objectives should be developed, monitored, reported and evaluated on an ongoing basis. Such information will help keep the city on track in meeting its vision for a sustainable future and is an important communications tool for residents. Further, trends analysis across the functional urban area should be developed in order to better understand and respond to metropolitan-wide issues.
- The city has a growing culture of participatory planning that should be strengthened through the regeneration process taking place in the city centre. The scope and scale of this regeneration will affect the city's development for years to come. It is anticipated that low-income residents in poor housing conditions will be rehoused. It is particularly important that these residents be included in the planning process.

Assessment and recommendations

In the late 1980s Poland transitioned from a centrally planned socialist state to a democratic market economy. Thus began a series of reforms that have significantly altered both spatial policy and the governance of land use in the country. Private land tenure was introduced and a new regulatory framework was established alongside decentralisation reforms.

Today, Poland has spatial plans at every level of government – national, regional and local – with each intended to inform the latter. Local governments regulate land uses and built form through local spatial development plans and give administrative decisions for development where none exist. Upper-level plans describe guidelines and inform and direct major national and regional investments. European Union (EU) directives have also shaped practices in some areas (e.g. environmental assessment) and EU funding has spurred on numerous public investments that influence land use. The legal and regulatory framework, together with institutional structures, the fiscal environment, legacies of built form, and socio-economic and political factors, all shape how land is used and developed at the local level in Poland.

While the following assessment relates to practices in Łódź, national legislative and regulatory frameworks shape instruments at the local level across Poland and are thus common to Łódź and other cities as well.

The current situation

Łódź is embarking on a major effort to reposition itself after facing severe economic and demographic challenges

Łódź is the third-largest city in Poland and is located about 100 kilometres south of Warsaw. Historically it was a prosperous textile centre, but has lost the majority of this industry to lower cost competitors in Asia. As a result, it has a large number of vacant late 19th through mid-20th century industrial buildings in the city centre. These are surrounded by former worker housing complexes, many of which are in need of significant repair and modernisation.

Further, like many cities in Poland, Łódź is experiencing the tandem effects of depopulation (due to low birth rates and outmigration) and deconcentration. Population projections suggest that by 2025 Łódź could lose 10% of its current population through a combination of natural decrease and outmigration. Consequently, even with economic revitalization, there is an expectation that the population of the city will continue to shrink.

Over time, people have left the city centre for newer housing developments on the fringe

Even prior to the end of socialist period, there were new housing developments constructed at the edge of the city. With the end of central planning and the restoration of property rights (including land), this process has accelerated and now the vast majority of the city population lives and works outside the historic city centre in newer housing units. New housing continues to be built even as the population shrinks, which has contributed to an increasing deterioration of older housing in the city centre and a concentration of low-income households in the area. Part of this expansion is related to an increase in the average size of homes.

Łódź is restructuring its economy and has had success with a new manufacturing role

Łódź has retained some of its textile capability but is now positioning itself as a light manufacturing centre that sits between the People's Republic of China (hereafter "China") and Western Europe. This location, combined with reasonably skilled and relatively low-cost labour, can provide the opportunity to import lower cost components from China for assembly into finished goods for the European market. There is also the future potential to import higher cost, more sophisticated components from Western Europe and assemble them for export to China. The city already has a dedicated train that travels from Łódź to China and back once every two weeks to move components and goods. However, most of the new manufacturing facilities have been built outside the city centre on greenfield land, including some on land in a special enterprise zone created by the Polish national government.

Transportation infrastructure improvements are vital to this hub function

To be successful as an intermediate processing and logistics hub, Łódź requires major improvements in rail and road infrastructure. Much of this is now being built, including better north-south and east-west roads and a significant upgrading of main-line rail infrastructure and terminal facilities in the city itself.

While much of the new infrastructure supports the movement of freight, there are also new passenger transport connections. In particular, the new fast rail line to Warsaw – a city which is expanding and becoming wealthier – could result in Łódź becoming a "bedroom" community in the future, if comparable housing units remain cheaper in Łódź.

New revitalisation and development and strategy

Łódź is hoping to restructure its economy and become a more compact city to better suit its smaller population and new economic function

With ongoing population decline, Łódź faces the challenge of providing public services across a fragmented territory, resulting in relatively high costs. Higher costs, or poor services, may make the city less attractive to the inward investment Łódź needs to accomplish economic regeneration. In addition, because the city owns land within the city centre, it has a particularly strong incentive to find a way to increase the value of this asset and thereby reap the benefits of higher land rents.

Constructing a compact city – a city that is more dense with less unused land – based on a revitalised urban core is also seen as having positive economic, social and environmental benefits. Social benefits include the opportunity to rehabilitate housing and allocate some of it to current low-income residents and to potentially revitalise urban neighbourhoods. Environmental benefits are seen as coming from the reduced use of private transport, reduced need for road construction and improvement, and a shift to public transport. The potential for these improvements resulted in Łódź receiving EU funds to support a major part of the investment in rehabilitating the core.

The strategy has great potential, but faces significant challenges

In order to be successful, Łódź will have to reshape the preferences of individual households and firms and reverse the current trend of dispersion. This will not be a simple task since the available tools are limited in number and scope. The majority of people now live outside the city centre and to date, firms have exhibited a preference for greenfield sites over infill brownfield sites in the centre. This means that repopulating the core with people and firms is most likely to come from new households and new firms, as opposed to existing ones. Moving current residents back is improbable because they have incurred significant costs at their new location that make them immobile. Similarly, existing firms are locked into their current location. Since Łódź must continue to provide services to these sites, they will continue to provide an alternative to a location in the urban core.

The shrinking demographic base is an impediment to the revitalisation strategy

Łódź clearly has the ability and authority to accomplish reconstruction given the financial support from the national level and the EU, but it faces the challenge of convincing firms and people to occupy the new developments. If the main source of new residents and firms in the revitalised core is new households without a pre-existing residence or a firm seeking a new location, then a declining population inevitably shrinks these numbers. On the other hand, if Łódź can make the core more attractive to households and firms than alternative locations, either in existing houses and buildings further out or new greenfield developments, then its strategy can be successful over time.

The city of Łódź owns a significant share of the land and buildings in the city centre and has a strong financial interest in increasing their value

The city administration is working to manage a shift in economic structure accompanied by a steady decline in population. It has embraced urban revitalisations as the main mechanism under its control to accomplish this and to manage its exposure to the costs of providing public services to firms and residents. In this regard Łódź has precisely the same incentives that most cities would face in similar circumstances. However, in Łódź the city also has the incentive as a large land owner to manage the development process in a way that increases the value of this asset. Arguably, doing so is in the public interest, because increased revenue from land in the urban core can be used to fund other services for residents.

There is the potential for tension between good public policy and the financial interest of the city. Even though it might be easier to extract revenue from tenants on city-owned land to fund other services, it might be more efficient and more equitable to fund these services from user charges so the beneficiaries pay directly. Perhaps the tension is best captured by considering the hypothetical question of how far the city administration will go in using its authority to ensure that the redevelopment policy is a success. Arguably, if the redevelopment strategy had been conceived of by the city but largely implemented by a private developer, the incentives for supporting the process would be different.

Land-use planning

Local spatial development plan coverage is very low…

Local spatial development plans are the key tool for local governments to shape urban form and use. They are the only legally binding plan which signals to residents, developers and investors how land, buildings and infrastructure will be developed in the future. However, plan coverage is low across most Polish municipalities and particularly low in Łódź.

In 2003, revisions made by the Spatial Planning and Development Act did not prolong the binding force of all development plans prior to 1994 (which were set to expire in 2000) since they had been established under a markedly different environment. This meant that a wide swath of cities would no longer have valid local spatial development plans – an issue that remains to this day. Since then, the adoption of new plans has been slow; the 2003 act did not designate the adoption of new plans as compulsory and there are several structural obstacles to the creation of new plans. For example, rules on property owner compensation for properties negatively affected by a local spatial development plan create a disincentive for municipalities to adopt them due to the potential for future litigation.

As a result, there is a reliance on the "planning decision" mechanism

Development in areas without a valid plan are governed by "planning decisions" for an individual building or change of land use requests. This can lead to fragmented and undesirable forms of development. Planning decisions are bound by national law and by specific legal procedures that limit planners' ability to direct development. For example, such decisions consider the existing features of buildings in the surrounding neighbourhood. If there is an existing building in the surrounding neighbourhood of a particular height, this provides the land owner the right to build a similarly-scaled structure. Thus, planning decisions are based on existing features, rather than desired ones. Further, there is no legal obligation for such decisions to comply with local spatial studies, which serve as the strategic planning document for municipalities. An overreliance on planning decisions in cities with low plan coverage can lead to new developments and uses which are costly to service and maintain, and may be contrary to the aims of broader spatial strategies. In effect, they facilitate sprawl.

Functional urban planning

While Łódź can manage development within its jurisdiction, it has no direct influence on adjacent municipalities

Łódź is part of a larger metropolitan system that links communes of varying size, population and wealth. Within the region (*voivodeship*), Łódź is by far the largest and wealthiest city, and has the most administrative capacity. The subset of municipalities in the region that are adjacent to Łódź tend to be strongly connected to the city in terms of employment flows, retail activity and their use of services provided in Łódź. Because of the high degree of interconnectedness there should be a strong interest in co-ordinated development.

However, while the regional authority can establish a development and planning strategy that cuts across the member municipalities, these documents are not enforceable, even if agreed upon. Moreover, since own-source revenue from households and firms is an important share of local government revenue, there is a strong incentive for completion among the municipalities for economic development. This includes new housing development and attraction of new businesses. As a result, "leap-frog" development is already occurring and if Łódź tightens its planning process to encourage development in the urban core, it risks losing even more households and firms to adjacent municipalities.

Free-riding by rural communes on Łódź's public services exacerbates the cost of service delivery

Increased development just outside the administrative boundary of a region is a common phenomenon in many OECD countries. The larger city may gain from an increased volume of economic activity, but if the individual firms and households do not contribute to the cost of the infrastructure and public services that residents are using, then both efficiency costs and equity issues arise.

This situation creates a dilemma for Łódź. On the one hand, it wants to achieve urban redevelopment and must rely on stronger spatial planning to encourage greater use of the core. On the other hand, tighter restrictions within the administrative boundaries of Łódź will increase the incentive for leap-frogging and damage the prospects for the urban redevelopment strategy.

The current structure only offers the possibility of a voluntary or collaborative solution for the dilemma

Under the current system of national planning and municipal governance Łódź has no capacity to play a direct role in the planning decisions of other municipalities despite any adverse impact it may experience from their decisions. In this setting, the municipality should try to establish close co-ordination and co-operation mechanisms with neighbouring municipalities even if they are not underpinned by an enforceable legal framework. OECD research has shown that metropolitan areas where such mechanisms exist have developed more compactly than those where they do not exist (Ahrend et al., 2014).

If Łódź has excess infrastructure and service delivery capacity, then it can benefit from additional use if it can collect additional revenue

Developing a broader metropolitan structure to deliver services could be advantageous for Łódź. This could provide a framework for joint funding of the services and because the extent and quality of services available are an important factor in the location choices of individuals and firms, such an agreement could also become a way to alter location choices. Clearly this only works if there is a win-win outcome for both parties, but since Łódź now lacks the ability to directly influence the development choices of its peers it must seek alternative pathways.

Recommendations

From the national down to the local levels, new legislation and emerging practices are leading to a more effective and participatory system of land-use governance. For instance, newly adopted national legislation has established a mechanism for metropolitan association – i.e. planning across a metropolitan area. Meanwhile, practices from Łódź indicate that the municipality is working to develop a sustainable and vibrant city in consultation with its residents. While there are many promising practices and reforms, some elements of the planning system undermine its effectiveness. The following points offer some guidance on how to make the planning system more coherent and robust for both the overarching system of land-use governance in Poland, and specificities related to the city of Łódź.

Łódź should fully explore the set of consequences associated with its revitalisation strategy

Łódź should undertake an assessment of the possible impediments and external shocks to its revitalisation strategy, and try to develop appropriate responses. To this end, there are several key considerations:

- How will the current low-income residents in the core be accommodated? Will they be housed in the core, or will be they be relocated to another location? In the case of relocation, what are the social and economic considerations and repercussions of such a move – e.g. access to employment, disruption of community-based social networks?
- What are the implications of the strategy for property values outside the core and how will this impact current owners? To what extent will the ongoing presence of a large stock of housing and proximate employment opportunities provide a viable alternative to a core location?
- To what extent is city-driven development through its own property in the core either an impediment to private sector development or a positive factor?
- Improving transport networks is a key part of the development strategy and improved connectivity is central for a logistics function, but better connectivity also allows easier outflows. This seems especially relevant given that Łódź is close to Warsaw and Warsaw is a much larger agglomeration that may come to absorb Łódź. How might this affect the city and its current strategy?

- How would the revitalisation strategy be affected if Łódź is successful in becoming an assembly hub and attracts new investment, but these firms demand locations outside the area Łódź has designated?

A co-operative approach to co-ordinating development and service delivery with surrounding communes offers the best hope for Łódź to achieve it development objectives

Łódź must play a lead role in building greater co-operation with surrounding communes. Łódź has both the greatest capacity to support co-operation and the greatest interest in seeing it become effective. But for co-operation to happen, all parties must perceive some benefits. In the case of Łódź this may require accepting that new development will occur in other municipalities but with agreements that free-riding on services provided by Łódź be resolved through an enforceable regional service delivery agreement.

Incentives for planning based on functional urban areas should be enhanced

Frameworks set at the national level in Poland have widely adopted the importance of planning based on functional urban areas and stress the need for integrated approaches. Such a lens is present in both the National Urban Policy in 2023 (2015) and the National Spatial Development Concept 2030. However, at the local level, there are a number of challenges to implementing such practices.

Local governments have a high degree of independence to manage their jurisdictional domains. While some governance structures exist to collaborate on transportation issues or shared services, these tend to be voluntary and to have limited functions. While local government competition can have benefits, such competition can also incentivise sprawl, as is seen in the case of Łódź and its surrounding locales. This can lead to an inefficient use of land, including adjacent developments with incompatible uses (e.g. animal husbandry next to residential developments), developments that are poorly linked to wastewater, sewage, waterline and transportation systems and infrastructure, and developments which are fiscally unsustainable to service.

The spatial strategies of urban and rural areas need to be coherently linked. The European Union's integrated territorial investments (ITI) in Poland encourage integrated spatial planning across functional urban areas. It is important that such investments be based on the good land-use practices that have been described in plans and strategies at the national, regional and local levels, such as developing brownfield sites in advance of greenfield ones, permitting developments only in areas where there is existing infrastructure to support them, and protecting agricultural lands, forested areas and watersheds. Through ITIs, municipalities are required to form collaborative bodies (municipal association agreements) in order to forward projects of metropolitan importance and to access investments. This mechanism has greatly facilitated municipal co-operation. It will be very important to institutionalise these practices in order to encourage such co-operation in the longer term (beyond the life of the ITIs). This could include special incentives for metropolitan co-operation such as dedicated funding streams for such projects.

However, where such collaborative planning is driven by voluntary local government associations, there is the risk that only certain types of issues – those that are less contentious and mutually benefit local actors – will be addressed, leaving substantive issues with little scope for action.

Different governance structures can help address such problems, for example the creation of two-tiered metropolitan government, the adoption of regional special purpose bodies, or greater involvement by regions in certain elements of spatial and sectoral planning. The recently passed Metropolitan Association Act (2015) offers yet another potential solution in this regard. It establishes a legal framework for metropolitan co-operation. For any such structure, the system of incentives and disincentives that are created should be assessed.

Polish municipalities are not alone in needing to tackle these issues. Metropolitan areas across OECD countries struggle to establish frameworks of co-operation to deal with joint issues that can last in times of both spending and constraint. OECD research has demonstrated the importance of overcoming such obstacles to find lasting co-operation. For example, an analysis of cities in five OECD countries found that those with fragmented governance structures tend to have lower levels of productivity (Ahrend et al., 2014).

Łódź has a growing culture of public engagement – better communication with residents and more opportunities for mutual decision making will enhance this function

Łódź has a growing culture of public engagement in decision making on spatial policy and land management. Given the pace of change in the city, it is increasingly important that public engagement practices be nurtured and strengthened so that citizens feel informed of and included in the changes that affect their daily lives. At present these practices are sometimes inconsistent, which sends mixed signals to residents. Related to this, communications information should be shared in a more accessible manner and greater efforts could be made to engage underrepresented individuals. This is particularly important as the city in in the midst of regeneration of socially deprived areas in the city centre.

Meaningfully involving citizens in decision making requires engagement at an early stage in the process (before decisions are locked in) as well as political buy-in, well-structured engagement activities, monitoring, evaluation and regular reporting. A central group (centre of expertise) to support such endeavours could help build this capacity.

The links between spatial and sectoral plans at the local level should be strengthened

Land use and development policies are connected to a wide range of other policy areas such as transportation planning, climate change adaptation and mitigation, and the provision of social services. Where strategies are integrated or aligned, they are likely to be more effective in meeting their goals. Presently, there is no general requirement that spatial plans be integrated with sectoral ones. However, the newly adopted Revitalisation Act (2015) encourages such integration in designated revitalisation zones, which is a promising practice and one that could be expanded upon.

Implementation of such an approach demands collaborative ways of working across departments. This requires a reorientation of day-to-day work practices. At present, OECD analysis indicates that different departments within one local government sometimes work at cross purposes. Integrated objectives, projects, monitoring, evaluation and communication can help realign such practices. It is particularly important that economic development plans and climate change strategies are linked to spatial ones and that such strategies are assessed and revised on a continual basis to ensure that they are reactive to changing conditions.

Local spatial development plan coverage should be increased and reliance on the planning decision mechanism should be reduced in the short term, and eliminated in the longer term

Local spatial development plans present an important signal to individuals and investors regarding how an area will develop into the future. They articulate a future planning vision and help mediate land-use conflicts before they occur. The low level of plan coverage in Łódź undermines these important functions.

Łódź has forwarded an integrated development plan which sets out its strategic goals to the year 2020; these include a sustainable and compact urban form and a flourishing city centre. It cannot meet these goals without the coverage of local spatial development plans and the abolishment of planning by decision. Since national rules shape this process, this is an issue for national reform as well.

Beyond plans, Łódź should also employ a broader range of tools, particularly fiscal ones, to manage the issues it is facing

Łódź should explore a broader range of tools that can be used for land-use governance. Planning is largely a tool that restricts choices. It can effectively block or constrain the actions of individual households and firms. But it does not alter preferences, which ultimately shape behaviour. In parallel with planning, there should be efforts to increase the attractiveness of the urban core to households and firms, but also recognition that many households and firms will continue to prefer an alternative location.

In addition to planning there is the possibility to use market forces directly, offer incentives that can alter preferences, use taxes or subsidies to alter the costs that individual firms and households incur with different decisions. For example, user fees are a market solution that could be explored as a way to address free-riding on public services. If these fees are differentiated for residents and non-residents of Łódź, they also provide a cost differential signal to location choices. As a major property owner in the urban core, the city could provide development incentives to private firms that invest in the restoration of housing or other types of buildings. Such incentives might include zoning variances, expedited building permission or other non-monetary factors that can trigger a change in preferences. Finally, there is the potential to use financial instruments in the form of taxes or subsidies to alter the costs of certain actions. In this respect Łódź is significantly constrained by Polish laws but it may be able to find specific charges or subsidies it can adopt.

Links between spatial planning and demographic, socio-economic, and fiscal analysis and forecasting will be critical for the city's resilience

The tandem trends of deconcentration and depopulation are well acknowledged in the city's spatial planning strategy. However, at present, the city is not meeting its goals in addressing these trends by reorienting land-use practices around a denser and more concentrated urban form which would facilitate infrastructure development and service delivery. There are institutional barriers to doing so and more tools are needed to meet these aims.

Given this, it is important that local spatial development plans, and above this the strategic "studies" that guide them, are effectively used to promote fiscal sustainability. Appropriate and effective land uses can ensure that residents have access to transportation networks, infrastructure and services. Land-use planning should make the most of existing services and corridors as opposed to opening up new areas to development, which will then require new public investments and ongoing upgrades and servicing. Municipalities with declining populations need to make the most of shrinking budgets. Coherent land-use strategies have an important role to play in addressing these challenges. In the longer term, the city may need to take such measures as decommissioning unused buildings or infrastructure.

Related to this, it is extremely important that land-use planning and an assessment of capital projects are linked. Capital projects are long-lived infrastructure projects such as water and wastewater, streets, community facilities or social housing. It is very common in municipalities for capital budgeting processes to be determined by engineers or financial analysts, but spatial planners should also be involved and decisions about capital assets should be made in conformity with spatial plans. This is critically important in Łódź where major investments are being made today that will impose significant operational costs in the future. The financial, social, environmental and spatial sustainability of the city must be considered in tandem, as one element impacts upon the other.

Indicators related to spatial development objectives should be developed, monitored, reported and evaluated on an ongoing basis

Łódź's spatial strategy describes the overarching development of the city based on three zones (inner, middle, outer). The city's spatial strategy would benefit from the development of key indicators that can be monitored over time to assess whether or not planning objectives are realised. In particular, Łódź seeks a more compact urban form and targeted density scenarios should be developed for each zone. Such indicators are an important part of policy formulation and will also communicate to residents whether or not key elements of the strategy are in fact being met. This pertains to rural areas as well – indictors should be created to monitor spatial planning objectives and report back to citizens. This may include indicators on changing land use, new investments and environmental protection.

The connection between the plans at different scales – national, regional, local – could be strengthened, particularly in the case of local and regional plans

Poland's multi-level system of spatial strategies and plans are meant to complement one another and mutually reinforce core objectives with higher order plans providing input and guidance to lower order ones. In practice, OECD analysis shows that the links between the three are sometimes inconsistent, and in particular, that regional spatial development plans are poorly linked to local ones; their co-ordination is limited only to public purpose investments of regional significance for which regional governments have purview. This lack of co-ordination across plans is one of the major spatial problems facing Poland.

As a whole, Poland's spatial planning framework can be made more effective by improving the integration of plans at different levels; introducing clear forecasting, monitoring and evaluation frameworks linked to strategic goals and objectives; and better communicating outcomes between governmental actors and to citizens.

Special infrastructural acts should be integrated into the planning system

The national government has created special infrastructural acts for public investment projects of national importance – e.g. major roads, railroads, airports and infrastructure development related to special events, such as the Euro Football Championships in 2012. These acts expedite significant projects. This has been instrumental in helping Poland to take advantage of investments funded through EU structural funds. However, these acts suspend common local planning law. They can be implemented even where they are contradictory to the aims of a local spatial strategy; they create special rules for expropriation; and they can bypass certain planning procedures (such as public engagement). While these acts were initially meant to be used for a limited time only (several years), they are now permanent. The ease of their application has created an incentive to use them. While originally intended to be used in extraordinary circumstances, projects forwarded under the acts are now commonplace. This mechanism is overused.

The function of these acts as a separate system should be examined. The way they are presently structured creates a parallel system that undermines the overarching planning framework, including confidence in due process. Regional and local authorities are not always well-informed of investments under these acts and investment decisions are not well-connected to local needs and conditions. In the short term, special infrastructural acts should be revised to limit their application to only necessary investments. In the longer term, these acts should be eliminated and developments should proceed through the regular planning system.

The system could be further strengthened by clarifying the right to develop **vis-à-vis** *property ownership rights along with the rules related to compensation rights*

The link between property rights and the right to develop in Polish law is ambiguous. These rights are not clearly defined in the 2003 Spatial Planning and Development Act and as a result, courts are adjudicating the right to development as a core component of property rights. Further, Article 36 of the Planning Act grants compensation to owners if they are negatively affected (i.e. the value of a property is reduced) by a local spatial development plan. This creates a litigation chill over the adoption of new plans.

Compensation rules create a disincentive for local governments to develop land-use plans. Better rules need to be developed regarding the issue of compensation. Specifically, compensation rights should be limited to specific criteria such as compensation in the event of land expropriation and to specific timeframes. Presently, the right to seek compensation has an unlimited timeframe.

Chapter 1.

Spatial planning in Poland

This introductory chapter details the spatial planning framework in Poland, including the roles and responsibilities of different levels of government, the types of plans at each scale, and the nature of local government revenues. It sets the scene for the case of Łódź that follows in Chapter 2.

Spatial planning in Poland has changed significantly over the past two and a half decades; the country has shifted from a centrally planned, communal form of land tenure under the socialist system to a decentralised and privatised system within a market economy. While this is a marked change, some elements of the system have retained their shape. For instance, during the socialist state period, spatial planning in Poland was also multi-level, but local governments were far less empowered than they are presently.[1] Today there are national, regional and local plans and higher order plans provide broad direction for lower order ones which are more detailed. Spatial policy at the national level sets out general goals and objectives related to the spatial development of the country and describes the general planning framework, including the competencies of subnational governments. At the subnational level, regional governments create more detailed plans and co-ordinate major public investments and finally, local governments forward local spatial development plans which have the highest level of detail regarding specific land uses, policies and practices. Local governments are the key actors for the implementation of spatial planning in Poland.

The Ministry of Economic Development is responsible for spatial policy on the national level which is described in the National Spatial Development Concept 2030 (*Koncepcja Przestrzennego Zagospodarowania Kraju 2030*). Regional governments (*voivodeships*) prepare regional spatial development plans for each region which offer a mid- to long-range perspective. Local spatial development plans at the municipal level (*gmina*) should be consistent with the aims and objectives of regional spatial development plans, though there is no enforcement mechanism to ensure compliance (i.e. compatibility of lower order plans with higher order ones).

Beyond the national and regional spatial strategies and plans, local spatial development plans are also affected by other national government acts and strategies related to the provision of key infrastructure (e.g. roads of national importance, rail lines) or the protection of culture, parks and heritage. Strategically important projects such as motorways, railroad lines or power plants are governed by their own special acts which suspend the common planning laws and regulations. Despite the presence of multi-scaled plans, local governments have a strong degree of autonomy in their planning functions. This is in line with the concept of subsidiarity, which argues that local issues are best handled by local authorities, including political decisions on matters of local importance. And so, there is a balance between the implementation of national and regional plans and local independence on matters of land use.

This chapter sets the overarching framework for the governance of land-use planning in Poland. It proceeds by outlining the national context for spatial planning followed by a description of the subnational tier of government and its distinct responsibilities, the overall planning system, other land-use regulations and policies which affect land use. This is followed by a case study of local spatial planning in the city of Łódź (Chapter 2) and finally, based on this case, an analysis of the major issues facing the governance of land management (Chapter 3).

Subnational government in Poland

Poland's contemporary system of spatial planning and governance is best understood through its historical evolution. After 40 years of highly centralised government throughout the communist period, "the reconstruction of local government became one of the first and most important pillars of the 1989 political transformation in Poland" (Kulesza and Szescilo, 2012: 485). The first municipal local elections (*gmina*) took place in the 1990s. Further decentralisation took place in 1998 when two levels of subnational government were created at the regional (*voivodeship*) and county/district (*powiat*) levels. In whole, the reforms consolidated the number of provinces or regions and created an intermediate tier of government between the national and local levels.

Box 1.1. A note on terminology

Spatial planning is a broad term used to describe the arrangement and processes for managing spatial development. Spatial planning is used to shape morphology and co-ordinate the spatial impacts of policies and decisions. This may include the location of key roads and other critical infrastructure or the protection of national parks and areas of cultural heritage. In contrast, the term land-use planning is narrower; it is focused on land-use regulation and development through policies and decision rules and is normally undertaken by local governments. This includes specific plans for parcels of land and how to use them, including decisions about the intensity and form that development takes.

The terminology used across countries can differ. In Poland, there are national and regional spatial development plans that give a high level of detail about spatial conditions and major public investments. However, they are structured more as framework studies than as comprehensive or integrated plans, such as in the US tradition. At the local level, Polish municipalities also establish local spatial development plans (*Miejscowe plany zagospodarowania przestrzennego*) for specific parcels of land. These may be referred to as land-use development plans or simply local area plans in other countries. See the Glossary for a list of terms used in this report.

For further discussion of land-use planning terminology, see Silva and Acheampong (2015).

Poland thus has three tiers of subnational government: *voivodeships* (provinces), *powiats* (counties or districts) and *gminas* (communes or municipalities) (Table 1.1). The *voivodeships* are based on historical regions for the most part; there are 16 of them. All told there are 379 *powiats* (including 65 cities with *powiat* status) and 2 479 *gminas*. Major cities, such as Łódź, can hold the status of both *gmina* and *powiat* (see Table 1.1 for a summary). Prior to this (1975-98) the administrative structure included over twice the number of regions (*vovoideships*) and the district/country level (*powiat*) did not exist.

As political and administrative bodies, there are some important distinctions between these tiers. The regional level includes both regional self-government and central government representation. The regional assembly (*voivodeship sejmik*) is directly elected for four-year terms.[2] The elected regional assembly can adopt and pass bylaws associated with its devolved responsibility and also elects a marshal (*marszałek*) and deputy marshal among its ranks. These positions form the executive of the regional government (referred to as the *zarząd województwa*).

Regional governments co-ordinate regional level planning, including infrastructure and cultural planning and environmental protection. They prepare regional spatial development plans and strategies for the whole territory of the *voivodeship*, but these are non-binding on municipalities, hence limiting their effectiveness. The regional level of government monitors, surveys and prepares reports on the state of subnational spatial development. The creation of a regional tier of government and its accompanying responsibilities was spurred by the process of accession to the European Union. Initially, regional policy in Poland focused on developing the objectives and principles of EU Cohesion Policy. In 2010, a framework for regional development was set out in the National Strategy of Regional Development. It enhanced the role for regional policy and the importance of forwarding approaches to spatial development that are coherent across sectors and mutually reinforcing across scales.

The central government is represented at the regional level by a governor (*voivode*), who is appointed by the Prime Minister. The regional governor is responsible for the administration of central government institutions and property and has powers in the areas of environmental protection, public safety and emergency preparedness.[3] The central government appointed governor acts as a check on the lawfulness of subnational government undertakings – region, county and commune (*voivodeship*, *powiat* and *gmina*).

Counties (*powiats*) are at a smaller territorial unit than the regional government and have an elected council, the head of which is the *starosta*. There are both rural (*powiat ziemski*) and urban (*powiat grodzki*) counties. Large urban jurisdictions are contiguous with county government – they are both *powiats* and *gminas*. They will herein be referred to as municipalities. Communes (*gmina*) are local government units with a directly elected council and a mayor.

Table 1.1. **Polish subnational political and administrative structure**

Governmental tier	Count	Political structure	Political executive
Regions (*voivodeships*)	16	Regional directly elected assembly (*voivodeship sejmik*) Regional representative of central government (*voivode*)	Marshal (*marszałek*) and deputy marshal elected among assembly's ranks form the executive office (the *zarząd województwa*)
County (*powiats*)	379 (including 65 cities with *powiat* status)	Directly elected council	Directly elected mayor
Commune (*gmina*)	2 479	Directly elected council	Directly elected mayor

Note: In large cities, the tiers of *powiat* and *gmina* are one in the same. There are three legal types of communes: 1) urban communes; 2) rural communes; 3) urban-rural communes.

A commune (*gmina*) or municipality can also create sub-units; these are not legal entities.[4] Their boundaries and competencies are determined by community councils. An English equivalent in the municipal context is a community "ward" or "quarter" formed by a general assembly of citizens; in a rural context these are equivalent to parishes.

Land-use planning is a major task of local governments. Local governments co-ordinate between the various spatial strategies pertinent to them; conduct operational planning and implement projects (e.g. urban regeneration); and determine important aspects of the regulatory framework for new buildings and developments. Local governments are responsible for determining their own spatial policies and for securing financing for public buildings and infrastructure (e.g. roads, sewage, water mains, schools, parks). Municipalities also collect property taxes and can determine the rates up to a threshold set by the national government along with other small taxes.

The municipal (*gmina*) tier is responsible for local spatial development plans and studies as well as a raft of decentralised functions related to the provision of services.[5] In contrast, regional governments are mostly responsible for strategic planning and regional development and have a much more limited role in service delivery. This spatial and regional development role has been strengthened with the influx of European Union structural funds. Regional operational programmes funded by the European Union are prepared by regional governments, which are also responsible for the final selection of projects to be financed.[6]

Local government revenues

Local government fiscal tools have the potential to shape land-use practices by creating spatial incentives or disincentives. For example, governments may provide a special levy to maintain agricultural land, establish tax exemptions to stimulate investment in brownfields, or create various incentives to include social housing in any new developments. The broader fiscal environment – such as fiscal transfers from other levels of government – affects how these tools are used and the demands upon them (Martin, 2015).

Local government revenues in Poland come mainly from four sources: 1) own-source revenues (levied through limited taxation powers in accordance with nationally determined maximum rates); 2) shares in personal and corporate income taxes; 3) general purpose grants; 4) conditional (or earmarked) grants. The latter may include resources from European Union budgets (structural and cohesion funds).

Local governments are the only subnational tier that holds the power to tax – though this power is limited. The property tax is the most important among these; it is levied on buildings and plots of land. The amount of the local taxes and fees is determined by each municipality but must comply with frameworks (and upper tax limits) determined by national legislation. Property taxes are generally levied on a square meter basis, with differential rates set for commercial versus residential buildings. For example, in the case of land, the property tax is based on the area of the land (to a maximum of PLN 0.89/m^2 of land); in the case of buildings it is based on their floor area (to a maximum of PLN 23.03/ m^2 of the usable surface of a building) (Ernst & Young, 2014: 91). This information is determined through the central registry and assessment takes place on an annual basis. Only one element of property tax is based on assessed value: certain construction structures (other than buildings) that are being used in an economic activity are taxed based on market value at a fixed rate (usually 2% of market value). Agricultural and forestry lands are subject to taxes which are separate from property taxes. Other taxes that are far more marginal to the municipal budget include taxes on agriculture lands (paid by hectare with soil quality taken into account), forests, large vehicles and a number of other minor duties.

Poland's tax on property as a percent of gross domestic product (GDP) is below that of the OECD average. Throughout 2000-13, tax on property in Poland as a percent of GDP remained relatively consistent and below that of the average for all OECD countries. It should be noted that these data are based on property taxation for all levels of government. In many countries (like Poland), property taxes are the sole purview of local governments, but in other cases, they are not.

Property tax revenues form a proportionately larger share out total revenues for rural subregions as opposed to urban ones (OECD, 2011a). Property tax revenue accounted for 28% of total budget revenues for predominantly rural subregions, 25% for intermediate subregions, and 17% for predominantly urban ones in 2014 (Government of Poland, 2015a). These figures have changed little since 2010.

Shares in central income taxes are allocated proportional to the amounts collected within the territory of the jurisdiction; there is no horizontal equalisation mechanism. These flow to regional, county and municipal governments, with municipalities receiving the largest share of the personal income tax transfer and regional governments receiving the largest share of the corporate income tax transfer. As such, there is a fiscal incentive for municipalities to increase their populations and for regional governments to foster business growth.

Figure 1.1. **Tax on property**

Total, % of GDP

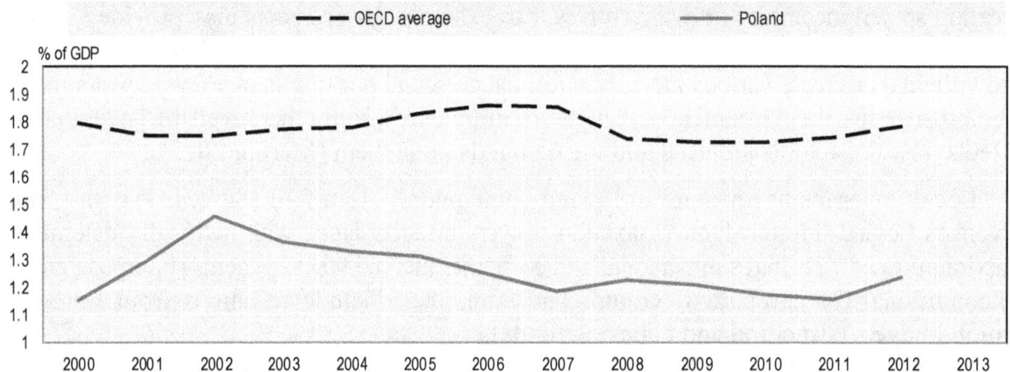

Note: Tax on property is defined as recurrent and non-recurrent taxes on the use, ownership or transfer of property. This includes taxes on immovable property or net wealth, taxes on the change of ownership of property through inheritance or gifts, and taxes on financial and capital transactions. This indicator relates to government as a whole (all government levels) and is measured as a percentage both of GDP and of total taxation.

Source: OECD (2015), "Tax on property" (indicator), http://dx.doi.org/10.1787/213673fa-en.

The general purpose grant for municipalities (subventions) consists of three parts: education, equalisation and balancing grants. Despite these delineations, municipalities can spend general grants at their own discretion – they are not tied to a particular purpose. The composition of each is outlined in the Act on Local Government Revenues.[7] Equalisation grants are financed through state budgets. Communes and municipalities whose per capita revenue-raising capacity from local and shared revenues is below that of a national threshold amount qualify for a basic grant determined on the basis of both population and tax capacity. The structure of the equalisation grant favours small municipalities with low population density (Sauer, 2013: 17).

Balancing grants distribute funds based on social expenditure; they take into account such issues as GDP per capita, the surface area of public roads per capita and the unemployment rate in an area. Regions also receive such grants, which are calculated on the basis of the unemployment rate, GDP per capita, area of public roads per capita and regional railways expenditure (OECD, 2008: 239). Some municipalities may also receive "compensating" grants, which are used compensate municipalities for lost property tax revenues due to special economic zones (special zones that can be established which provide businesses with income tax rebates, hence limiting tax intake).

The final group of grants (conditional or earmarked) are related to the responsibilities that have been delegated to local governments; the most important of these are provisions for social assistance. The vast majority of intergovernmental transfers in Poland are lump sum as opposed to matching grants. Grants from the EU are included under conditional or earmarked grants in most cases. The value of local governments' revenue to GDP ratio in Poland has been significantly higher than the average of EU countries (Uryszek, 2013: 253).

It bears noting that the recently adopted Revitalisation Act (2015) expands municipal fiscal instruments on two points: 1) it enables local governments to calculate and collect an adjacency levy (at a rate higher than that set by general rules), which can be used to capture the increase in value of real estate as a result of the construction of municipal infrastructure in the regeneration zone; 2) it introduces the possibility to increase the real estate tax rate (up to PLN 3/m^2 of land per year) in the designated revitalisation zone for new developments.[8]

National spatial planning: The overarching framework

As with the structure of subnational government, the legislative framework for spatial planning in Poland has changed significantly over the past 25 years. Three major pieces of legislation have shaped the planning environment. The 1984 Spatial Planning Act enhanced local governments' ability to shape physical planning and embark on new economic opportunities. This act was replaced in 1994 by one which updated the scope and practice of local planning to operate in the context of a transitioning market economy. The 1994 act was then replaced in 2003 by the Spatial Planning and Development Act, which outlines the present regulation and conduct of land use and spatial planning.

The 2003 Spatial Planning and Development Act (along with its secondary legislation) regulates the development of spatial policies and spatial plans (concepts, plans, studies) and divides various powers among the administrative tiers of government. It also discusses the mechanisms through which to engage the public in the development of spatial plans and how to resolve conflicts between parties (citizens and local government). Governments at the national, regional and municipal levels create spatial plans, but county level governments do not.

The spatial plan prepared and adopted at the national level is the National Spatial Development Concept 2030 (NSDC). It presents an assessment and analysis on the state of spatial planning in the country and puts forward a vision for the country's spatial development to the year 2030. As such, it is both a document which offers an assessment of key challenges and guidance on how to co-ordinate and implement public policies that have a significant territorial impact (see Box 1.2 for a summary of the key objectives). Substantively, the national spatial policy is a means to inform regional strategies and mutually align their core objectives around the goals of sustainable development.

The NSDC is a basic co-ordination measure of spatial policy at the national level in Poland that involves checking the compliance of a regional spatial development plan for each *voivodeship* with the NSDC. This is done by the minister responsible for regional development whose approval constitutes an obligatory part of a legal procedure on the elaboration and adoption of a regional spatial development plan. However, it is not an internally binding document. It is the purview of the Council of Ministers to decide the extent to which the NSDC will inform government programmes (and be binding upon them).

The NSDC takes a dynamic view of spatial effects – remarking that interventions should not be delivered according to a traditional view of locales as rural versus urban, but rather on the basis of analysing socio-economic and spatial characteristics. This is described as a "functional areas" approach to policy development; it recommends that regional governments base their analyses on functional areas (as opposed to administrative boundaries or urban/rural dichotomies). In this regard, the NSDC has been informed by the European Union's Cohesion Policy and by the OECD's approach, including its 2008 *Territorial Review of Poland*, which called on governments to adopt a functional understanding of rural-urban dynamics and linkages (Szlachta and Zaucha, 2010; OECD, 2008).

Box 1.2. **Objectives of the National Spatial Development Concept 2030**

The six objectives outlined in the National Spatial Development Concept 2030 are:

1. to improve the competitiveness of Poland's major urban centres in the European context through functional integration while preserving the pro-cohesive polycentric settlement structure
2. to enhance internal cohesion and balance the territorial development of the country across regions by promoting functional integration, creating conditions for spreading development factors, multifunctional development of rural areas and using the internal potentials of all territories
3. to improve Poland's connectivity in different dimensions by developing transport and telecommunications infrastructure
4. to develop spatial structures supporting the achievement and preservation of Poland's high-quality natural environment and landscape
5. to enhance the resistance of spatial structures to natural disasters and loss of energy security and to develop spatial structures supporting national defence capabilities
6. to restore and consolidate spatial order.

Source: Government of Poland (2012), "National Spatial Development Concept 2030: Summary of the government document", www.esponontheroad.eu/dane/web_espon_library_files/682/national_spatial_development_concept_2030_summary.pdf.

The strategy sets out a desired policy agenda and proposes future reform. Its sixth objective – to restore and consolidate spatial order – offers a number of ways in which to improve upon the present system of spatial planning. These include: "introducing an integrated (coherent and hierarchical) socio-economic and spatial planning system at different governance levels, re-organisation of regulations ensuring efficiency and universality of the spatial planning system, strengthening of institutions and improving the quality of spatial planning" (Government of Poland, 2012).

Beyond such overarching goals related to the multi-level governance of spatial planning, the strategy also describes specific practices, such as the need for legal regulations to develop brownfields in advance of greenfields (and to permit greenfield development only where brownfields are fully developed) and minimum standards for infrastructure provision and access to services (Government of Poland, 2012). It advocates that local government studies should be binding, not only for the local spatial development plan, but for all administrative decisions related to development and that local governments should be obliged to develop plans for areas undergoing intense development and adopt provisions to prevent "scattered development". It further recommends the implementation of a system of ongoing monitoring and evaluation. At present, the planning documents of lower level governments should be compliant with higher level plans but the criteria of such compliance are ambivalent and there is no legal basis for harmonisation between thematic plans. The NSDC in essence forms a "wish list" of suggested reforms to be introduced by an act of parliament at an unspecified future date. It offers a signal to local governments of best practices that should be adopted, with no regulatory ability to shape land-use practices.

The NSDC is composed of several documents, including a Resolution of the Council of Ministers. Several maps indicate the spatial orientation of the national approach in general terms. These are organised by theme and give a high-level view of spatial development priorities among such topics as: the development of functional urban areas, commuting patterns, agriculture, the transportation network, oil and natural gas developments, water management, electricity grid infrastructure, conservation areas, renewable energy resources, and the coverage of local spatial development plans. These maps are at a scale of 1:2 500 000. National spatial plans at this level of detail are common across OECD countries. The maps they contain are used for illustrative purposes and not to make land-use decisions (for which a far greater level of detail would be needed).

The national level has recently adopted a complementary document to the NSDC – the National Urban Policy in 2023 which was adopted by a Resolution of the Council of Ministers (2015). This document is oriented around the goals of sustainable development and improved well-being, and both offers a diagnosis of issues affecting urban areas in Poland and sets strategic objectives and accompanying actions for implementation. It identifies the key challenges facing urban areas in Poland as follows:

- to create compact, friendly, low-carbon and energy efficienct cities
- to improve spatial development in urban areas and prevent suburbanisation
- to more effectively use the potential of urban centers and their functional areas to create growth and jobs and sustainable development
- to prevent socio-economic and spatial degradation of urban areas
- to improve the quality of management and co-operation in urban areas
- to develop transport infrastructure, including public transport in urban areas.

Implementable actions to address these issues include legal amendments, the creation of knowledge centres to share best practices and expertise, and directions for the use of EU funds on the 2014-20 funding period. Each of the implementation actions identifies the minister responsible, the required actions, and monitoring and assessment of the implementation/reforms. This document builds on analysis of the OECD's *Urban Policy Review of Poland* (2011b) and is the product of two years of discussions between various stakeholders (businesses, communities and experts) and public consultations.

Special infrastructural acts

Poland has adopted a number of so-called "special infrastructural acts" (*specustawy inwestycyjne*) pertaining to different types of infrastructure development – e.g. railroads, public roads, airports, liquefied natural gas terminals and anti-flood buildings. All of these special acts define specific local rules pertaining to the development of specific infrastructure projects. They create separate criteria for such projects and suspend any application of local planning, with the exception of environmental assessments. There is also a Special Act for Nuclear Power Plants, but it has come under broad criticism by local governments and has not been used (and apparently will not be used).

The ministry, acting through the *voivode*, can enact a local spatial development plan instead of a municipality if a local plan is adopted that contravenes national and regional infrastructural interests. This clause has only been used in one instance, where it was applied to power lines, which did not at the time have a special act. The government does not draw on this function because it can instead use special acts to develop major public investment projects.

Table 1.2. **The spatial planning environment: Level of government, strategies and legislation**

Level of government	Planning authority	Legislation	Strategy or study	Plan
National government	Ministry of Economic Development	Spatial Planning and Development Act (2003)	– National Spatial Development Concept 2030 – Sectoral and government programmes – National Urban Policy in 2023	
Regional government (*voivodeship*)	Regional assembly and executive (marshal)			Regional spatial development plan
County government (*poviat*)	County council and executive (governor)		No guidelines pursuant to the Act on Spatial Planning and Development	No legal requirement to develop a plan
Local government (*gmina*)	Municipal council and executive		Spatial study (*Studium uwarunkowań i kierunków zagospodarowania przestrzennego gminy*), not an act of local law but binding on municipal authorities in developing plans	– Local spatial development plan (*Miejscowy planzagospodarowania przestrzennego*), legal ordinace – Public investment strategy (voluntary plan)

Source: Own elaboration.

The adoption of special infrastructural acts was spurred by EU membership and access to infrastructure funds. With this infusion of funding Poland found that it needed special acts in order to develop critical infrastructure and to support major events (i.e. Euro 2012). Almost all new roads have been built using these acts. Special infrastructural acts speed up the public investment process from an average of six years to two years.[9] Presently, all critical infrastructural investments are covered by such acts. Investments made under special acts do not need to conform to the Spatial Planning and Development Act, thus making it is possible to develop a project that is contrary to local plans.

Special infrastructural acts create unique mechanisms for land expropriation; the Constitutional court has described the acts as dangerous, but considers them temporary to facilitate strategic investment. However, most of the acts have been amended to remove their sun-set clause, in effect making them permanent. A new law is presently being drafted (named the "Strategic Public Investments Act") that would revoke six of the special infrastructural acts, establish expropriation and administrative decision rules, and create an end date of 2023 for the acts.

Other spatial planning policies and regulations

While the 2003 Spatial Planning and Development Act and the National Spatial Development Concept 2030 set the overall framework and objectives for planning, there are a number of other acts and regulations which also affect the local planning and regulatory environment.

One of most recent among these is the Metropolitan Association Act (9 October 2015) – adopted largely to address the need for public transport across functional urban areas. Under the act, metropolitan associations can be formed in an area inhabited by at least 500 000 inhabitants that includes a city with county rights as well as the seat of the governor or the regional council of the province. Further, the act stipulates that such metropolitan associations should conform to the national spatial plan, consider the functional relationships between the various bodies it will represent and may only proceed on the basis of majority consent.[10] The controlling body of the association is to be composed of delegates from municipalities and counties included in the union with a management board consisting of three members, elected by the assembly. The activities of any such association are to be financed through a portion of the personal income tax and municipal contributions.

The government has also recently adopted the Revitalisation Act (9 October, 2015), which specifies the legal basis for the revitalisation of degraded areas (e.g. legal definition, stakeholders, procedures for strategic documents). Importantly, such areas are defined both in terms of their physical features (i.e. infrastructure and buildings) and their socio-economic characteristics.[11] By enacting the "revitalisation area procedure", municipalities can draw on special rights and planning tools (see Box 1.3 for further details).

The Building Law (1994) describes the procedures for building permissions along with various technical requirements for buildings and structures. The Real Estate Management Act (1997) contains detailed rules on property management, (sub) division and merging; this includes details on the fees that may be collected by public authorities in the development of urban infrastructure. The Environmental Protection and Management Act (2001) stipulates the regulation of environmentally protected lands. It sets the framework for other regulations pertaining to the protection of forests, water and wastewater management, and the protection of nature or arable land.

A number of other acts make reference to the Spatial Planning and Management Act and contain regulations pertaining to the development, usage and protection/conservation of specific kinds of lands or assets. These include acts on wildlife conservation, public roads, paid motorways, geological and mining activities, the consolidation and exchange of agricultural plots, energy law, forestry, the protection of cultivatable land and conservation of forest soils, maritime areas and maritime administration, inland waters, national sanitary inspection, monument protection and preservation. Acts pertaining to environmental protection and culture and heritage create governmental bodies such as the Nature Conservation Officer and the Monument Conservation Officer. In the context of cultivable land protection, water management, flood control, territorial waters, health resorts and national defence, the relevant minister and regional *voivode* bear an enforcement and monitoring role.

Spatial planning in Poland has been shaped by priorities set forward by the European Union – as is evident with the creation of special acts spurred by an influx of EU infrastructure funding. The European integration process led to significant legal/administrative reform in Poland throughout the 1990s and into the early 2000s and has helped shape the regulatory framework for environmental protection. For example, the current Strategic Environmental Assessment model was prepared for the purposes of EU accession and membership.[12]

While the European Union gives member states a free hand in their spatial planning systems, it does forward strategic documents about infrastructure and nature preservation that can inform local planning.[13] For example, the EU's Natura 2000 established a network of protected bird and habitat sites that are identified as special areas of conservation or special protection areas by member states. This includes both lands that are considered nature reserves and thus limit human activities and those which allow them within a sustainable management regime. Natura 2000 designated lands are identified in local spatial development plans.

Box 1.3. **Revitalisation Act, 2015**

Cities across Poland have adopted programmes of revitalisation for degraded areas over the past decade, many of which have been located in central historical districts. Drawing on these experiences, the newly adopted national legislation establishes both the mechanisms and parameters for such revitalisation projects. Degraded areas are determined based on the presence of a combination of social challenges along with economic, environmental or technical problems. Once determined by the governing parameters, the designation as a "special revitalisation zone" allows a municipality to draw on special rights and planning tools and implement a local revitalisation plan (modified local plans). It also makes it possible to ban zoning decisions and introduce a general pre-emption rule. Key features of the act include:

- Social tenement housing as a category of public purpose. The act extends the category of "public purpose" to social tenement housing projects in the zone area. This enables municipalities to expropriate private property for this goal. Social housing projects must meet three conditions: they must be supported by public funds; be constructed by a non-profit developer; the resulting flats must be distributed based on non-market principles.
- Faster administrative procedures. The act simplifies the procedures for relocating tenants in order to rebuild flats. Such a decision can be made by the *voivode,* out of court. The interests of tenants are still protected; there must be a new/temporary flat reserved for relocated tenants and tenants must be reimbursed for their removal costs. New administrative rules also make it easier to expropriate real estate in cases of uncertain ownership.[1]
- Zoning decisions banned and pre-empted. The act permits municipalities to exclude all, or a portion of, zoning decisions within the designated revitalisation zone. It also permits the municipality to enact pre-emption for all properties in the zone.
- Financial refunding of real estate claims. It allows the municipality to compensate owners of real estate on the basis of replacement property, as opposed to offering financial compensation.
- Building renovation. In instances where a municipality owns at least 50% of a property, it can force building renovation. Other part-owners, after a court decision, will be required to participate in the costs of renovation. It also establishes a provision whereby the municipality can support the renovation of private property up to a threshold of 50% of the cost of the project.
- Simplification in public procurement. The act makes it possible to simplify the public procurement procedure when the cost of investment is lower than the EU threshold. A municipality can levy the tender procedure if the procurement serves to support local residents and entrepreneurs. This procedure must be transparent and secure equal rights for subjects that want to receive procurement.
- Higher real estate tax rate for not complying with the local plan. Local authorities can increase the real estate tax rate for owners who do not realise the investments foreseen in local plan. Four years after enacting the local plan, the tax rate increases to a maximum of 3 PLN/m².

Note: 1. Under the new rules, a municipality does not need to submit compensation through a court deposit in such cases. If a rightful owner if determined, the municipality has three months to pay compensation for the real estate in question, as determined by the court.

Source: Ustawa z dnia 9 października 2015 r. o rewitalizacji, Dziennik Ustaw Rzeczypospolitej Polskie, http://dziennikustaw.gov.pl/du/2015/1777/1.

Regional spatial planning

The regional level (*voivodeship*) has a somewhat limited role to play in spatial planning. The regional spatial development plan is, in form, much like the National Spatial Development Concept 2030. It is a strategic document and does not directly inform infrastructure planning because of the special infrastructural acts which presently govern this process. There are no legal tools at the regional level to establish land-use planning regulations.

While the spatial plans (i.e. National Spatial Development Concept 2030 and regional plan) are meant to be "nested", there is in fact no enforcement mechanism. The regional plan outlines investments of national and regional importance and general development conditions. It also demarcates the regional settlement system, protected areas and functional areas important for the whole region and defines closed (e.g. military) areas, areas with the potential to flood, and grounds with mining resources, all of which require special treatment. The regional level acts mostly as an advisory body in planning; it may give opinions on local spatial development plans. Regional spatial planning is developed through a formal and largely closed process and there are no advisory bodies which inform its development. This limited consultation reduces buy-in to the resulting plan.

The *voivode* – the legal representative of the central government in the region – is responsible for controls and audits and for some policy functions. The *voivode* has control competencies over all levels of government including every act of law that is issued by the regional self-government and local governments. He/she assesses local plans for their principles of legality and can make a claim against a municipality which would then be settled in the administrative court in the case of a legal or procedural error.

The *voivode* does not create policy; policy creation is a competency of regional self-governments, namely the marshal, who has jurisdiction over planning at the regional level and some regional laws (such as the Act on Tourism). But the marshal (regional self-government executive) does not give structured advice to the municipalities. Taken together, the regional level offers strategic advice and analysis through the marshal and control and audit of legal procedure for land-use plans through the *voivode*.

While the regional level has a limited role in spatial planning due to the principle of subsidiarity, it is playing an increasingly important role in managing funds from the European Union which have spatial implications for public investments (regional operational programmes, ROP).[14] Over the 2007-13 period, regional governments across Poland managed approximately 25% of all EU funds, while over the 2014-20 funding period this will increase to 40% (Flanders Investment and Trade Market Survey, 2014). ROPs are prepared and implemented by a management board (the regional self-government executive, marshal's office) within each region based on a regional development strategy which prioritises investments and decides on projects.[15]

The planning system at the local level

Local governments are the main actors in Polish land-use planning. Three tools presently shape land-use planning at the local level: spatial studies, local spatial development plans and planning (or development) decisions. Each will be described below in turn.

Spatial studies

The first tool, spatial studies, form a kind of master plan for development in a municipality or local government (*gmina*), but they are not an act of law. These spatial studies are referred to in the Planning Act as "Study on the conditions and directions of spatial development" (*Studium uwarunkowań i kierunków zagospodarowania przestrzennego gminy*). They are a legislated (obligatory) framework study used to guide local planning policy in municipalities in the preparation of local spatial development plans. Local spatial development plans should be consistent with spatial studies, but the study itself is not a legally binding document on local spatial planning. Spatial studies provide an analysis and commentary on a range of social, economic and demographic issues that affect local planning and cover the entire municipal area.

Local spatial development plans

In contrast, local spatial development plans are legally binding documents (*Miejscowe plany zagospodarowania przestrzennego*); they are an essential planning document for an area. The procedures for their production and adoption, including their scope and forms of documentation (e.g. types of maps/illustrations), are outlined in the Spatial Planning and Development Act 2003. Local spatial development plans are future-oriented documents. They prescribe particular permissible assignment of land uses and detail the size and volume of permitted development, rules for property division, and the protection of cultural assets and heritage buildings for a given area in a municipality. The plans also estimate infrastructure costs (e.g. roads) and detail property expropriation that would result from their development.[16] Since 2008, plans also require a strategic environmental assessment.

Plans are prepared by the municipal executive (city president, mayor or *wojt* – i.e. chief magistrate in a rural commune) and adopted by municipal councillors. The ordinances outlined in local spatial development plans are the only legal mechanism that local governments have to determine development boundaries and direct permitted uses. By law, all members of the public have the right to participate in the process of developing local plans; basic participatory procedures in the preparation of the plans are legally prescribed. Draft local spatial development plans are made public for comment and review for a minimum of 21 days. The local community is invited to submit comments, which are then considered (accepted or rejected) in the final drafting of the plan. The rejected comments are subject to vote by the council as the plan goes up for approval (vote by council). Beyond the prescribed rules for public participation, there is also an appeals process; the procedural and administrative legality of local spatial development plans can be appealed to the *voivoid*, *voivodeship* or national administrative courts. In the case that such an appeal is successful, the process for the development plan must start anew.

Building regulations and "change of use" are outlined in the Spatial Planning and Development Act 2003 and in the Building Law. It is upon the onus of developers to prove compliance with the necessary requirements. There is no right to develop associated with land ownership. Enforcement powers related to the local spatial development plan and compliance with building codes falls on the district or country level (*powiat*), which in the case of larger cities (i.e. Łódź, a city with *powiat* status) is one and the same as the municipality.

Planning decisions

The Spatial Planning and Development Act 2003 was adopted to address a number of perceived failures in the existing system, namely the lack of existing plans and a cumbersome planning process. The changes to the act did not prolong the binding force of all development plans prior to 1994 (which were set to expire in 2000) since they had been established under a markedly different environment. This meant that a wide swath of cities would no longer have a valid local spatial development plan – an issue that remains to this day. In 2013, only 28% of the country was covered by a valid local spatial development plan (Kowalewski et al., 2013). In order to ensure that new developments could proceed in the absence of valid land area development plans, a simplified administrative mechanism was continued under the 2003 legislation – planning decisions.[17]

Planning decisions are not required to be consistent with a local government's planning study, which sets out the conditions and directions for development. They are a special administrative procedure. Planning decisions are made for building approvals, change of land use and for the location of a public investments. For example, for residential developments on a greenfield location where there is no valid local spatial plan, three requirements would need to be met for a permit to be issued: 1) at least one nearby plot needs to have a house on it (where the proximity between the two is not clearly defined); 2) the land must be accessible by public roads; 3) existing infrastructure must be sufficient for the project.

Planning decisions are a controversial measure. They can create an incentive for disjointed development and are a procedure that runs parallel to the planning system as a whole, and often with contrary aims. In many municipalities, planning decisions are credited with leading to poorly co-ordinated developments and sprawl (Radzimski, Beim and Modrzewski, 2010; Halleux, Marcinczak and van der Krabben, 2012).

Summary

Spatial and land-use planning systems create various incentives and disincentives for the governance of land use. In Poland's case, the spatial policies at the national, regional and local levels (and binding local land-use plans) are not always well co-ordinated. Further, the legal framework protecting home/land owners creates a clear disincentive against the creation of up-to-date land-use plans at the local level due to the potential for litigation against local government in cases where property values are negatively affected by a plan. The fiscal tools at municipalities' disposal are presently weak in directing urban form. Finally, major infrastructure investments – particularly an influx of EU cohesion funds – are reshaping urban-rural spaces. However, there few incentives for municipalities to work together despite this being a clearly articulated value of national and regional spatial strategies.

The national government defines the spatial planning system through acts of law; it prescribes how regional and local governments will carry out their respective functions, the relationships between levels of government, planning processes and interactions with citizens. It has also forwarded a spatial strategy (NSDC) for the whole country. It puts forward an agenda for reform. These provide signals for regional and local governments to react to and evolve towards. Regional governments are required to prepare spatial strategies to guide development. The compliance of a regional spatial development plan

Figure 1.2. **Local spatial planning procedure**

The process for adopting municipal plans and studies

Intention	Announcement of intention to draft plan, including descriptions of how and when to submit proposals to the plan or study (minimum timeframe 21 days)
Notification	Formal notification to institutions regarding the intent to develop a local plan or study
Proposal review	Review and consideration of submitted proposals
1st draft	Draft of plan or study
Feedback	Feedback from relevant institutions
Formal agreement	Formal agreement for changing land use from agricultural or forest to non-agricultural or forest.
2nd draft	Second draft prepared
Public review	Public review including open house discussion, and public review period (30 days minimum for studies; 21 days minimum for plans)
Comments collected	Collection of public comments (14 days minimum for plan; 21 days minimum for study)
Vote	Voting on plan by municipal council
Procedural assessment	Assessment of plan against procedural and legislative requirements by Voivode governor. If passed, the plan is legally binding; if failed, an assessment by the Voivode governor, the plan is rejected.
Official gazette	The plan is legally binding after the promulgation in the Voivodship Journal of Laws (official gazette)

Note: Sequentially, the spatial study (or the "Study on the conditions and directions of spatial development") should be carried out in advance of land-use plans such that the former may inform the development of the latter.

Source: Own elaboration.

for each *voivodeship* is checked against the NSDC. This is done by the minister responsible for regional development, whose approval constitutes an obligatory part of the legal procedure for the elaboration and adoption of a regional spatial development plan. These regional plans have the capacity to play an important role in forwarding a functional view of regions – something that the National Spatial Development Concept 2030 advocates. The resulting plans at the local level should be consistent with this approach. However, there is no binding mechanism to ensure that this is the case. As such, the incentives for the spatial alignment and co-ordination of plans are largely voluntary.

The national government has created special infrastructural acts for infrastructure projects and planning for events which are of national importance. Such acts are used to decrease the time that it would otherwise take such projects to be approved; they also suspend common local planning law and limit local public engagement in decision making. In essence, such acts create a parallel planning system for important public projects.

The planning system creates incentives for local governments to develop spatial studies that analyse ongoing social, economic and demographic trends that have spatial implications for how a city develops in the future. Local spatial development plans – plans for specific areas of a city – are meant to take into account the analyses provided by spatial studies; however, this is non-binding. At the same time, the 2003 Planning Act negated the validity of plans created prior to 1994 and continued the tradition of a parallel system of planning decisions to address areas with no valid plan coverage. This mechanism – planning decisions – limits the city's ability to direct development and has dominated the planning process. It can be said to incentivise "one-off" decisions based on limited criteria to direct usage and, as a consequence, incentivises scattered developments that may or may not conform to the objectives outlined in spatial studies.

The Polish Civil Code defines property rights as one of the main rights of citizens. The Spatial Planning and Development Act 2003 (*Ustawa o planowaniu i zagospodarowaniu przestrzennym*) defines an owner's rights to develop. Property can be used and developed by a property owner if the plans meet local land-use plan requirements and, where there are none, by meeting planning decision requirements. Judicial decisions recognise development rights as a core element of property rights. This statement forms the basis for compensation – if development rights are limited, the administrative court may interpret this as a limitation on property rights. Local land-use plans are the most important planning instrument to shape the direction of future developments. However, as has been mentioned, plan coverage is low in most cities. There are several reasons for this – e.g. time, capacity – but one of the major issues that has hampered the adoption of new plans is the possibility of land owners to seek compensation in the event that the value of their land is negatively affected by the adoption of a land-use plan (as outlined in Article 34 of the Spatial Planning and Development Act 2003). This right has no time limit and creates a litigation chill and unknown cost consequences over the adoption of new plans.

Presently, municipalities largely rely on patchy zoning policies to manage development; they have limited fiscal tools to shape land-use practices. Municipalities have the authority to levy taxes on real estate (land and buildings) along with other small taxes and fees. Real estate taxes can be levied up to a threshold set by the national government. However, land-use value-capture instruments, brownfield redevelopment incentives, historical rehabilitation tax credits and a swath of other such fiscal instruments are rarely used.

The national spatial strategy, along with regional plans, describes the importance of analysing jurisdictions through a functional lens to best structure public investments and promote co-operation and collaboration between municipalities. In practice, there are few incentives for municipalities to adopt such a view through their own planning processes. Such engagement is largely voluntary, with the exception of some funding agreements which stipulate requirements for local government co-operation. However, this is changing. The EU's ITI instruments Poland to encourage integrated spatial planning across functional urban areas and the new Metropolitan Association Act (2015) established a new institutional mechanism to solidify such co-operation.

Poland's spatial policies and regulation of land have changed significantly since the country's independence. Over this time, the institutional features and acts of law governing land use and regulation have changed. Locally elected governments were established and the return to a market economy ushered in an influx of private capital which has transformed municipalities and communes. These changes brought the return of land rent, the privatisation of land and buildings, growth in urban policy making, and a vastly reconfigured system of social services. Poland's accession to the European Union in May 2004 was also formative in spurring a number of reforms, including new environmental laws (e.g. environmental assessments) and the creation of special infrastructural acts to facilitate the influx of structural funds. As will be further discussed in Chapter 3, this evolving system has a number inadequacies which the case study of Łódź will highlight (Chapter 2).

Notes

1. During the socialist period, spatial planning was performed at three levels and some provisions establishing the hierarchy of planning documents were specified by the Spatial Planning Act of 1984. After transition and reintroduction of local government in 1990, the leading role in the planning process was given to communes/municipalities. From that moment on, the role of local authorities and social participation in the planning process has consistently increased over time.

2. The main mode of interaction between central and subnational governments is through the Joint Central-Local Governments Committee (*Komisja Wspólna Rządu i Samorządu Terytorialnego*). Its task is to consider issues related to the functioning of local government and state policy towards self-government, as well as issues concerning local self-government within the sphere of action of the European Union and international organisations. Local governments are represented on the committee by their respective associations. This body is governed by an act (Act of 6 May 2005 on the Joint Commission of Government and Local Government and the representatives of the Polish Committee of the Regions of the European Union). The Joint Commission consists of 12 representatives of the government and the 12 self-governments. The Council of Ministers and other entities responsible for the preparation of draft legislation, programmes and other governmental documents concerning issues of local government are required to present them to the Joint Commission for its opinion on these documents, together with a forecast of their effects. The Joint Commission appoints permanent teams. This group meets less than once every two months.

3. Competencies at the regional level for environmental protection are subject to the General Directorate of Environmental Protection (national level), not to the *voivode*.

4. In rural areas such a unit is called a *sołectwo* in the case of villages; in towns they may be referred to as *dzielnica* (city quarter) or *osiedle* (city settlement).

5. These decentralised functions include: pre-school and primary education (for children up to 15 years old); "communal services" such as water and sewage, solid waste collection and disposal, street lighting, local parks and green areas, central heating; local road and street maintenance; local public transport in cities; communal housing; voluntary fire brigades; various social services; cultural and recreation facilities; and local (spatial) planning.

6. European structural and investment funds include the European Regional Development Fund (ERDF), the European Social Fund (ESF), the Cohesion Fund, the European Maritime and Fisheries Fund (EMFF), the European Agricultural Fund for Rural Development (EAFRD).

7. Education grants are the largest among these; their allocation is determined by the minister responsible for education based on a number of criteria.

8. New developments are defined as those that were not built in a period of four years from the date of the entry into force of the plan.

9. Based on an assessment provided by interviewees.

10. The Metropolitan Association may be created by the Council of Ministers on its own initiative or at the request of the concerned municipality or county. In both instances, association requires a majority vote of 70% in the case of municipalities and towns with country rights and 50% in the counties.

11. The act stipulates that the revitalisation area may contain up to 20% of the municipal territory and a maximum of 30% of its residents.

12. The legal base for environmental assessment in Poland dates back to the Environmental Protection and Management Act of 1980; however, this act lacked specific standards for environmental impact assessment procedures (Mackowiak-Pandera and Jessel, 2006: 202). In 1999, the new local government act delegated responsibility for environmental impact assessments and strategic environmental assessments to regional and local governments. The current framework is outlined in the 2001 Environmental Protection Act. There are also provisions related to public participation and environmental impact assessment and SEAs in the 2003 Land-Use Planning and Management Act.

13. This may even include aesthetic judgements – for example, Poland recently ratified the "Landscape Act" in fulfilment of its European Landscape Convention requirement (ratified by Poland in 2004), which regulates the presence of advertisements in public space.

14. The role of the regional level is described in Article 38-45 of the Spatial Planning and Development Act 2003.

15. The website for the Łódź region project office is: www.rpo.Łódźkie.pl.

16. The only possibility to expropriate is when the "public purpose" is concerned (though the law does not specify if public or private financing is involved). There is a specific catalogue of such investment (e.g. roads, communication, gas transmission, water supply).

17. The planning decision mechanism was not new in the Polish law, but established in 1994 and continued by the 2003 act.

Bibliography

Ernst & Young (2014), "Poland: The real state of real estate", *The Polish Real Estate Guide: Edition 2014*, Ernst & Young, www.ey.com/Publication/vwLUAssets/EY_Real_Estate_Guide_Book_2014/$FILE/EY_Real_Estate_Guide_Book_2014.pdf.

Flanders Investment & Trade Market Survey (2014), *European Funds, 2014-202 in Poland*, Flanders Investment & Trade, http://www.flandersinvestmentandtrade.com/export/sites/trade/files/market_studies/249141020151357/249141020151357_1.pdf

Government of Poland (2015a), "Revenue of gminas and cities with powiat status budgets, 1995-2014", *Local Data Bank* (database), https://bdl.stat.gov.pl (accessed 25 March 2016).

Government of Poland (2015b), Revitalization Act of November 9 2015 (in Polish), http://dziennikustaw.gov.pl/du/2015/1777/1 (accessed 25 March 2016).

Government of Poland (2012), "National Spatial Development Concept 2030: Summary of the government document", Ministry of Regional Development, Warsaw, www.esponontheroad.eu/dane/web_espon_library_files/682/national_spatial_development_concept_2030_summary.pdf.

Halleux, J.M., S. Marcinczak and E. van der Krabben (2012), "The adaptive efficiency of land use planning measured by the control of urban sprawl: The cases of the Netherlands, Belgium and Poland", *Land Use Policy*, Vol. 29/4, pp. 887-898, http://dx.doi.org/10.1016/j.landusepol.2012.01.008.

Kowalewski, A. et al. (2013), Raport o ekonomicznych stratach i społecznych kosztach niekontrolowanej suburbanizacji w Polsce, Fundacja Rozwoju Demokracji Lokalnej, IGiPZ PAN, Warsaw.

Kulesza, M. and D. Szescilo (2012), "Local government in Poland", in: Moreno, A.M. (ed.), *Local Government in the Member States of the European Union: A Comparative Legal Perspective*, INAP, pp. 485-503.

Mackowiak-Pandera and B. Jessel (2006), "Developments of SEA in Poland", in Schmidt, M., Joao, E. and E. Albrecht (eds.), *Implementing Strategic Environmental Assessment*, Springer Berlin Heidelberg, pp. 201-215.

Martin, I.W. (2015), "What property tax limitations do to local finances: A meta-analysis", *Working Paper*, No. 12, UCLA Research on Labour and Employment, University of California, Los Angeles, http://escholarship.org/uc/item/4cw578fp#page-2.

Ministerstwa Administracji i Cyfryzacji (2015), Sejm przyjął ustawę o związkach metropolitalnych, https://mac.gov.pl/aktualnosci/sejm-przyjal-ustawe-o-zwiazkach-metropolitalnych (accessed 25 March 2016).

OECD (2015), "Tax on property" (indicator), http://dx.doi.org/10.1787/213673fa-en (accessed 5 October 2015).

OECD (2011a), "OECD regional typology", OECD, Paris, www.oecd.org/gov/regional-policy/OECD_regional_typology_Nov2012.pdf.

OECD (2011b), *OECD Urban Policy Reviews, Poland 2011*, OECD Publishing, Paris, http://dx.doi.org/10.1787/9789264097834-en.

OECD (2008), *OECD Territorial Reviews: Poland 2008*, OECD Publishing, Paris, http://dx.doi.org/10.1787/9789264049529-en.

Radzimski, A., M. Beim and B. Modrzewski (2010), "Are cities in Poland ready for sustainability? Poznań case study", *REAL CORP*, 2010 Proceedings/Tagungsband, Vienna, 18-20 May 2010.

Sauer, S. (2013), "The system of local self-government in Poland", Research Paper No. 6/2013, Association for International Affairs/Asociace pro mezinárodní otázky.

Silva, E.A. and R.A. Acheampong (2015), "Developing an inventory and typology of land-use planning systems and policy instruments in OECD countries", *OECD Environment Working Papers*, No. 94, OECD Publishing, Paris, http://dx.doi.org/10.1787/5jrp6wgxp09s-en.

Szlachta, J. and J. Zaucha (2010), "A new paradigm of the EU regional development in the context of the Poland's National Spatial Development Concept", *Institute for Development Working Papers*, No. 001/2010, Sopot, Poland, www.instytut-rozwoju.org/WP/IR_WP_1.pdf.

Uchwała Nr 218/2008. Prezydium Państwowej Komisji Akredytacyjnej z dnia 10 kwietnia 2008 r, http://a.umed.pl/procesbolonski/materialy/PKA_kryteria_studenckie.pdf.

Uryszek, T. (2013), "Financial management of local governments in Poland: Selected problems", *Journal of Economics, Business and Management*, Vol. 1/3, pp. 252-256, www.joebm.com/papers/55-X00017.pdf.

Chapter 2.

The governance of land use in Łódź

This chapter details the major land-use challenges in Łódź along with how land uses are governed and regulated. It starts by describing the city's demography and economy and how they have changed over time along with a description of the built environment and major land-use pressures. This is followed a discussion of the governance arrangements and the planning tools at the city's disposal to shape land uses and the pattern of incentives and disincentives that they create along with other regulatory measures. The relationship between Łódź and its rural environs is explored and finally, the major land-use issues and challenges facing the city are presented.

This case study of planning issues and practices in the city of Łódź illustrates the numerous challenges and opportunities facing an area undergoing rapid transformation. Łódź is shifting from a former industrially dominated economy towards a service-oriented one. It is a dynamic city. The area is seeing major investments in transportation infrastructure and is in the midst of a large urban regeneration project spurred by an influx of EU structural funds. It is also a city experiencing demographic change – namely population aging and outmigration – and at the same time, deconcentration/sprawl.[1] All of these factors, along with a myriad of others, affect and are shaped by urban form.

Rural communes surrounding the city are also changing. Despite ample available land within the city boundaries, rural communes such as Nowosolna are experiencing growth in residential housing, business/industry development and agricultural intensification. New road infrastructure is opening some areas to new developments, further transforming land uses and the built environment. These developments require careful planning so as to ensure that land uses do not conflict with and detract from one another.

This case study of the Łódź illuminates promising practices driven by a vibrant community of engaged politicians, public servants, academics, businesses and industry associations, non-governmental organisations (NGOs) and citizens. However, it also reveals contradictions which are embedded within the present spatial planning system. In particular, the existence of a parallel system of planning decisions which undermines local development objectives and incentivises sprawl; a disconnect between nationally mandated regional plans and that of local ones; low local plan coverage and a legal framework that discourages further plan development; growing, but inconsistent, public engagement practices.

In effect, Łódź and its surrounding commuting areas do not have the adequate tools to shape the visions of development articulated in both regional and local spatial strategies. The tandem trends of deconcentration and depopulation facing Łódź, along with rapid investment and redevelopment in the urban core, make the need for effective spatial planning all the more pressing.

Placing Łódź in context

Łódź is the capital (and largest) city of its namesake region (Łódź Voivodeship).[2] Łódź sits in central Poland, just over 100 kilometres from the capital city, Warsaw (Figure 2.1). It is in this sense ideally located. The city stands at the cross roads of two major highways: the existing and planned sections of the country's main north-south and east-west highways and metropolitan expressways. It has an international airport and railway connections that are in the process of expanding. It is the fourth most populous metropolitan area in Poland after Katowice, Warsaw and Krakow.

The city has changed greatly over the past two centuries. Once a small agrarian town, Łódź grew rapidly in the 19th century spurred by the clothing and textile industries, which led to its moniker "Polish Manchester." This heritage is visible today with impressive industrial structures towering over the landscape; unlike Warsaw, Łódź's built environment was not destroyed during the Second World War. The population, however, dramatically changed over this period. Prior to the Second World War, the population of Łódź stood at 672 000. Over the duration of the war, the city lost approximately 200 000 inhabitants. By 1988, the population had grown to 854 000 inhabitants. Today the population of the city of Łódź stands at 706 000 (2014).

Figure 2.1. **Functional urban areas of select cities in Poland, by population, 2014**

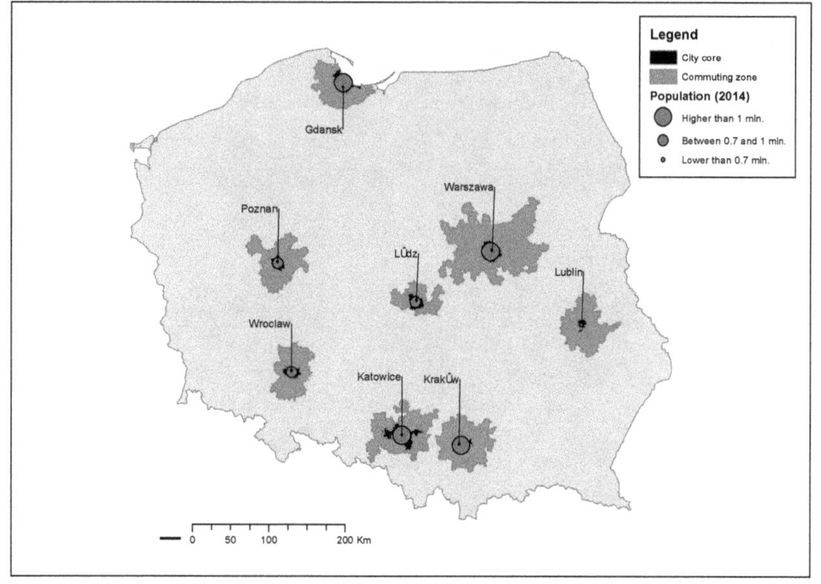

Source: OECD (2015), *OECD Metropolitan Areas Database*, Metropolitan eXplorer, http://measuringurban.oecd.org.

The demographic profile of the Łódź region (*voivodeship*) indicates that the population as a whole is getting older and shrinking in terms of overall size (due to a combination of outmigration and low birth rates). The region has, and will continue to have, the highest share of persons aged 65 and over as a percent of population of any region in Poland (Figure 2.3). In 2010, the old age dependency ratio for the region stood at 21%. It is estimated that this will increase to 40% by 2030; a figure that is only surpassed by the Świętokrzyskie region to Łódź's south (at 41% in 2030). Population projections for the Łódź region to the year 2050 by age grouping further elaborate these demographic trends. The region's share of population aged 64 and over was 17% in 2015; this is expected to increase to 34% by the year 2050 (Figure 2.4). Over the same period, the share of individuals aged 15 to 64 is expected to decline from 68% to 54% over the same period.

Like the region as a whole, population levels in the city of Łódź are also expected to decline in the coming years due to a combination of low birth rates and outmigration – from 706 000 in 2014 to 668 500 in 2020 and down to 638 000 by 2025 (Statistical Office in Łódź, 2014a). Thus, by 2025 Łódź will potentially lose close to 10% of its current population. Łódź is experiencing a faster rate of population decline than other comparable Polish city.

Figure 2.2. **Total population, Poland and Łódź**

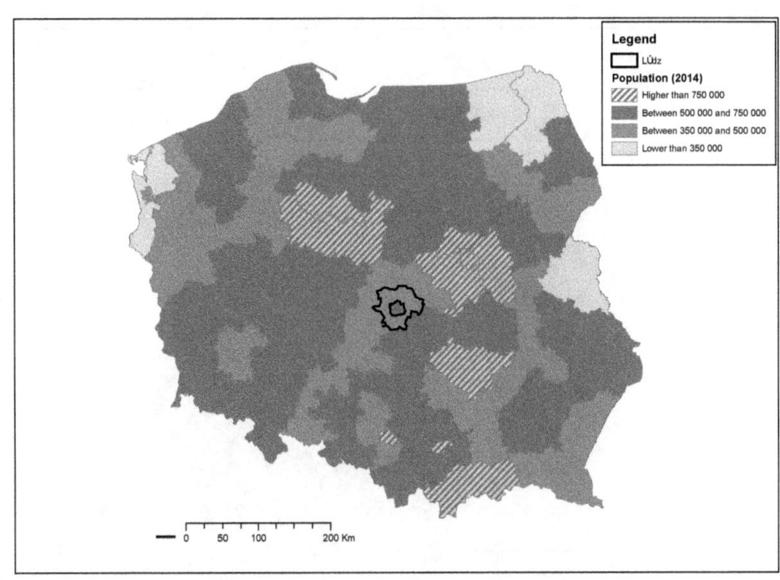

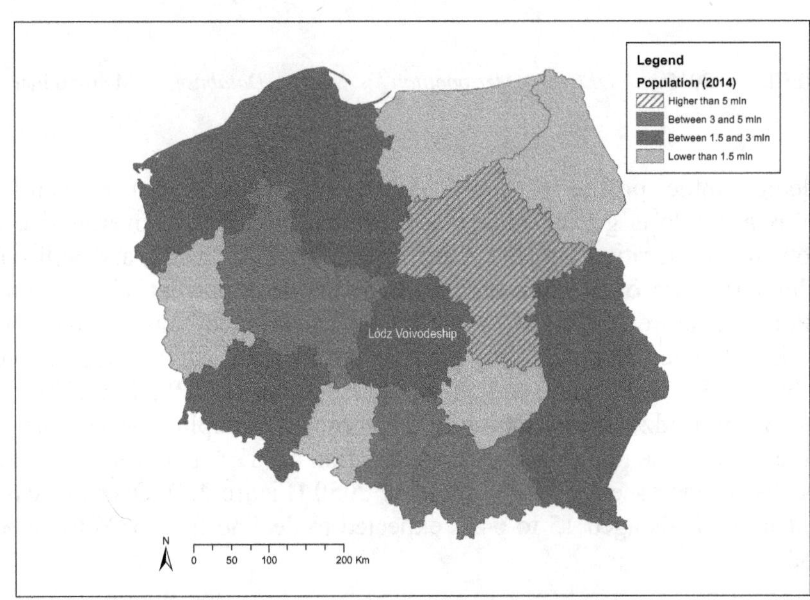

Notes: The figures above show OECD territorial units classed by small regions (Territorial Level 3 or TL3) and regions (Territorial Level 2 or TL2).

Source: OECD (2015), *OECD Metropolitan Areas Database*, Metropolitan eXplorer, http://measuringurban.oecd.org.

The working age population accounted for 61% of the inhabitants of Łódź in 2014. Both the share of the population in retirement age and the share of the population of pre-working age show an increasing trend (Statistical Office in Łódź, 2014a). As a consequence, the demographic dependency ratio (the number of non-working age population per 100 persons of working age) is increasing: it increased from 62 at the end of 2013 to 65 at the end of 2014 (Statistical Office in Łódź, 2014a).

Figure 2.3. **Elderly dependency ratio, Łódź region**

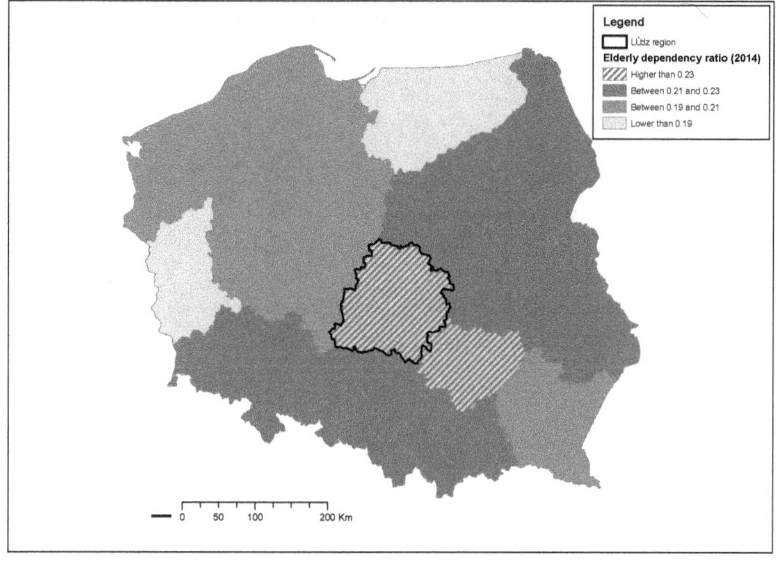

Notes: The figure above shows OECD territorial units classed by regions (Territorial Level 2 or TL2). The elderly dependency rate is defined as the ratio between the elderly population and the working age (15-64 years old) population.

Source: OECD (2015), *OECD Metropolitan Areas Database*, Metropolitan eXplorer, http://measuringurban.oecd.org.

Figure 2.4. **Łódz region, population projection by age grouping**

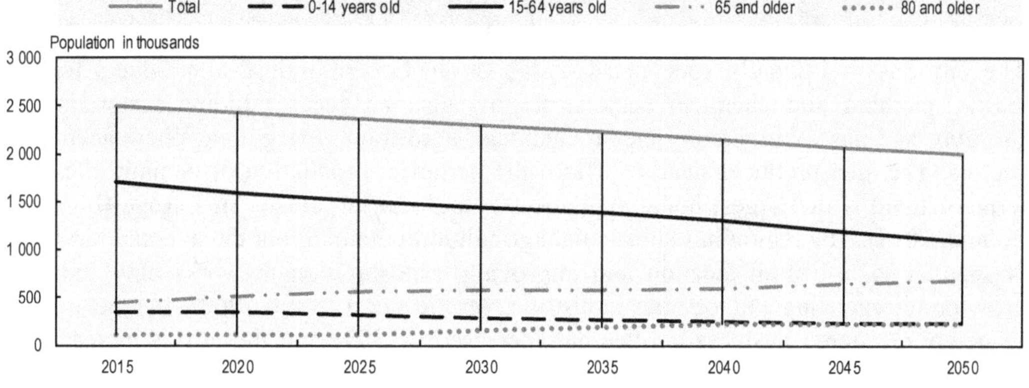

Source: Central Statistical Office of Poland (2014), "Population projection 2014-2050", http://stat.gov.pl/en/topics/population/population-projection/population-projection-2014-2050,2,5.html.

The unemployment rate in Łódź remains relatively high compared to other Polish cities of a similar size (approximately 12% compared to approximately 5%) (Statistical Office in Łódź, 2014a). The city's residents have a lower average life expectancy than that of other Polish metropolitan areas (three years less for women and five years less for men) (Statistical Office in Łódź, 2014a).[3] Łódź's poverty level is lower than in districts surrounding the Łódź metropolitan area, as reflected by the rate of children under the age of 17 whose parents receive the family benefit against the overall number of children at this age.[4]

Table 2.1. **Łódź: Key indicators**

Population, labour market, land, economy

Population:	
2014	700 600
2020 projected	668 500
2025 projected	638 000
Population per km² (2013)	2 426
Non-working age population per 100 persons of working age (2013)	62
Unemployment rate (2013)	12.3%
Average monthly gross wages and salaries in PLN (2013)	3 710.91
Agricultural land as a percentage of city area (2013)	41.7 %
Forest cover as a percentage of city area (2013)	9.4%
GDP per capita:	
Łódź (2013)	131.0
Poland (2013)	122.1

Source: Statistical Office in Łódź (2014a), *Statistics of Łódź 2014*, http://lodz.stat.gov.pl/en/publications/statistical-yearbook/statistics-of-lodz-2014,1,11.html.

After years of single industry dominance and its subsequent decline, Łódź's economy has been diversifying and the services sector now accounts for approximately 70% of all employment in the city (Statistical Office in Łódź, 2014a). The city has a number of educational institutions, including the University of Łódź, a technical school, a medical university, arts and music academies and is home to the national film school. It is in a large part because of this that the city experiences a positive balance of migration for those aged 20-29 years (of approximately 700 people per year). It is also home to important healthcare, cultural and entertainment facilities and, as the seat of both regional and local governments, has a fair amount of employment in the public administration.

Despite growth in the services sector, Łódź also remains a place of manufacturing. The city has traditionally specialised in the production of industrial products for the textile, clothing and chemical sectors. It now also produces building materials and furniture and has a burgeoning electrochemical, agro-food, energy and pharmaceuticals sectors. The area produces nearly 70% of the domestic production of ceramic tiles and terracotta and is the largest home appliances manufacturing cluster in Europe (Invest in Poland, 2015). The region has substantial agricultural potential, but the average farm size is small. Łódź's central location and improving transportation networks have led to a growing warehousing and logistics industry. Over the past 12 years (2003-14) the number of newly registered business entities has increased by 30% and the city is increasingly successful at attracting foreign capital (Statistical Office in Łódź, 2014a).

The built environment and changing urban form

Łódź's landscape, form and architecture bear the hallmarks of a post-industrial and former socialist city (Figure 2.5). Leading on from 19th century clothing and textile production, the socialist state period saw intensified industrialisation. This accompanied social-spatial stratification with higher income individuals residing in the centre of the city and lower income individuals concentrated in suburban and peripheral zones. Later era social policy reversed this trend. New housing estates were constructed in the 1960s and 1970s and higher income residents moved to the suburban areas of the city while lower income residents increasingly concentrated in the central parts.

Over the past decades Łódź's traditional clothing and textile industry has collapsed. Upon Poland's transition to a democratic state in 1989, Łódź experienced rapid economic decline and the unemployment rate ballooned to over 25% in the mid-1990s. Over this period the city experienced high levels of outmigration and urban poverty increased. Many of the city's old industrial plants fell into disrepair and came to form vast areas of post-industrial ruins along with uninhabited houses. These features of the landscape constitute huge challenges for the revitalisation of the city today. But while many of these impressive industrial structures are now derelict, many have been renovated into stunning condominium housing or have been turned into shopping malls or arts centres. The "Manufactura" complex – a large arts/leisure/business/hotel development – is a prime example of how such spaces can be transformed. Łódź's urban form is a study of contrasts. There are industrial areas throughout the city, with concentrations in the north-east and south-west, as depicted in Figure 2.5.

Figure 2.5. **Industrial areas in Łódź**

Source: Own elaboration.

State-led housing construction declined after Poland gained independence and the private market saw growth in the demand for private detached homes. Cities across Poland experienced the height of such suburban development around the 2000s. There has also been growth in condominium developments. Thus, suburban locales have a decided mix of socialist state era, condo and private detached homes. This phenomenon of deconcentration is similar to that seen across other Central Eastern European countries.

While many post-socialist cities experienced a rapid urban development in their core in the 2000s, this was not the case in Łódź. Inner city renewal programmes over this period had little effect and the share of dilapidated tenement houses rose dramatically as maintenance responsibilities were passed down from public agencies to lower income residents (Marcińczak and Sagan, 2011). This has created social-spatial inequality. For example, sociologists from the University of Łódź have identified "enclaves of poverty", defined as areas in which the percentage of households receiving social assistance benefits exceeds 30% (Warzywoda-Kruszyńska et al., 2013; Warzywoda-Kruszyńska and

Golczyńska-Grondas, 2010). The majority of such enclaves are concentrated in the city's downtown in degraded housing.

Today the city has four main types of housing stock. There is the historic urban core (inhabited by 21% of the population) which is a multifunctional area with 19th and 20th century tenement houses, historic villas and palaces as well as post-industrial architecture that currently is being used as housing, commercial and office facilities. The second major type of housing stock are post-war communal flats (mono-functional housing areas).[5] The third major housing type is single-family housing concentrated in suburban areas of the city and finally, the fourth are areas of new housing development which are totally detached from the city centre (e.g. Olechów). Łódź has a relatively high percentage of apartments from the 1970s and relatively fewer from 1989 to 2002 compared to other cities across Poland. Older housing stock tends to be in the poorest condition (City of Łódz, 2010).

A 2005 assessment of housing conditions classed approximately 75% of the city's residential buildings as being in "poor condition" (City of Łódź, 2010). Łódz is not alone; "underhousing" or inadequate housing is an issue facing much of Poland. Figures from 2015 estimate that 15% of the population resides in substandard housing conditions (Habitat for Humanity, 2015). Further, 44.8% live in overcrowded conditions, in contrast to the EU average of 17% (Habitat for Humanity, 2015).

Housing in Łódz is relatively affordable compared to that of other major cities, but this is in large part because it is of lower quality. In comparison to the five other largest cities in Poland, Łódz has the lowest average prices per square meter of housing and lower average rental rates for figures going back to 2007 (Narodowy Bank Polski, 2016: 9). To give an idea of relative prices, figures from the first quarter of 2016 indicate the average price of an apartment in Łódz to be PLN 185 000 – this stands in contrast to the average prices in Kraków (PLN 273 000), Gdansk (PLN 275 000), Poznan (PLN 300 000) and Warsaw (PLN 446 000) for the same time period, which were all significantly higher (Expander, 2016). However, this figure does not account for the quality of the housing. However, quality-adjusted pricing (hedonic price index) paints a more accurate picture of housing; between 2008 and 2015, the year over year quality-adjusted price index for price per square meter of housing in Łódz has roughly followed the six-city average (Figure 2.6). Therefore, while the housing may be more affordable compared to other cities, this is likely because it is of a lower quality.

Łódź is experiencing increasing development in suburban areas and beyond in adjoining rural communes. There is growing traffic congestion in the city and it is estimated that 100 000 people travel into the city from the surrounding commuting zone on a daily basis. The OECD's Sprawl Index provides one comparative assessment of this phenomenon (shown in Figure 2.7). The Sprawl Index measures growth in the built-up functional economic area adjusted for growth in the city population. By this measure, Łódź's functional economic area had the highest Sprawl Index in 2006 of any comparable functional urban area across Poland (Figure 2.7). The assessment by functional urban area – as opposed to administrative unit – facilitates comparative analysis.

At present, built-up urban form covers nearly half of the city's area and forest coverage amounts to almost 10% of its total area – the largest of these is the Łagiewnicki forest in the northern part of the city (approximately 1 200 ha). However, figures from 2012-13 indicate that the amount of agricultural and forested land in the municipality declined over this time while the amount of urbanised land increased (Statistical Office in Łódź, 2014a).

Figure 2.6. **Quality-adjusted housing price index (hedonic price index)**

Price in PLN per m² of housing, growth quarter compared to the same quarter in the previous year

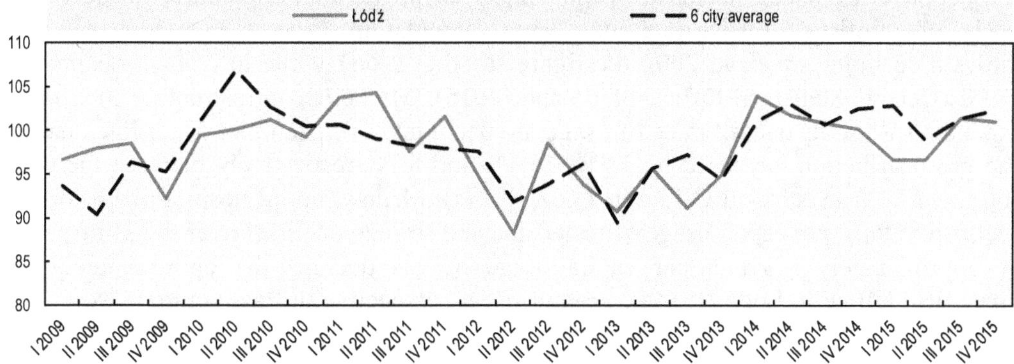

Note: Six-city average based on the following cities: Gdańsk, Gdynia, Kraków, Łódź, Poznań and Wrocław.

The hedonic price index corrects for quality changes (e.g. increase or decrease in the share of more expensive housing in the sample); the hedonic index takes into account changes in the quality of housing in the analysed sample in each quarter, thus differs from a simple average (i.e. the mean price).

Source: Narodowy Bank Polski (2016), *"Information on home prices and the situation in housing and commercial real estate market in Poland in 2015 Q4".*

Figure 2.7. **Sprawl Index, functional boundary and urban core, 2006**

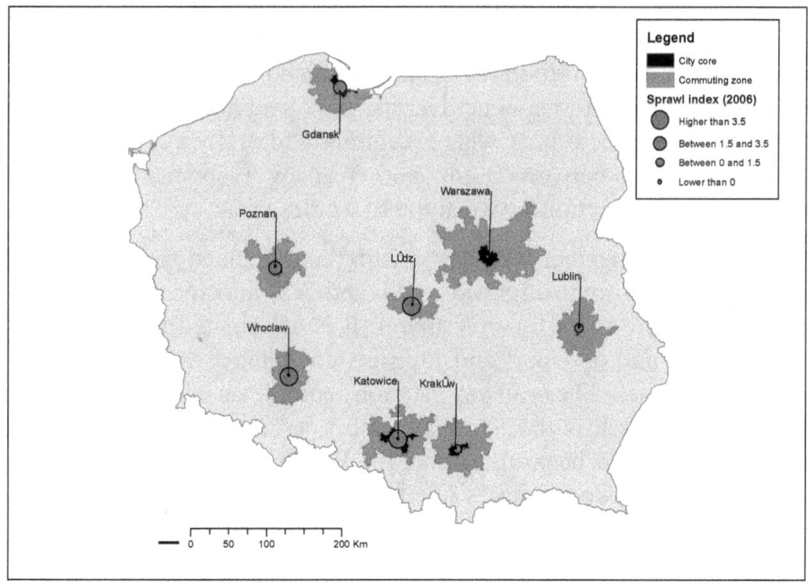

Notes: A functional urban area is characterised by a densely inhabited "city" and a "commuting zone" whose labour market is highly integrated with the cores. This methodology makes it possible to compare functional urban areas of similar size across countries. The Sprawl Index (SI) measures the growth in built-up area adjusted for the growth in city population. When the city population changes, the index measures the increase in the built-up area relative to a benchmark where the built-up area would have increased in line with population growth. The SI is equal to zero when both population and built-up area are stable over time. It is bigger (lower) than zero when the growth of built-up area is greater (smaller) than the growth of population, i.e. the city density has decreased (increased).

Source: OECD (2015), *OECD Metropolitan Areas Database*, Metropolitan eXplorer, http://measuringurban.oecd.org.

The combined trends of deconcentration and depopulation place pressure on infrastructure and services. Over the past 12 years (2003-14), the number of dwellings per 100 people in Łódź has increased by almost 9%, while the total population has decreased by 11.4% (Statistical Office in Łódź, 2014a). Population density (population per km^2) shows a declining trend; in 2002 the figure stood at 2 667 while in 2014 it declined to 2 408 (Central Statistical Office of Poland, 2015). Municipal infrastructure in Łódź is expanding while its overall rates of usage are declining. For example, water line, sewage and gas distribution increased by 7.5%, 25.3% and 8.3% respectively between the years 2005 and 2013 (Statistical Office in Łódź, 2014a). Meanwhile, per capita usage of each declined in turn: per capita usage of water line and sewage declined over the same period by approximately 5% and per capita usage of gas declined by approximately 6% (Statistical Office in Łódź, 2014a). From a fiscal perspective, infrastructure is expanding while the ability to pay for it (per capita transfers and user fees) is declining.

The hinterland of Łódź's functional urban area is seeing far more land-use change than that of its core. Over the period 2006-12, land use in the core changed by 1.89% while in the hinterland of the functional urban area it changed by 7.82%.[6] The largest contributors to the land-use change in the hinterland stem from increases in industrial and commercial land uses (1.98%), road and rail developments (1.62%), and construction sites (1.51%).

This discussion of Łódź's changing urban form is not complete without mentioning several large-scale transportation projects which are presently transforming the city. An influx of EU and central government funds is remaking the city into a transportation hub, which strengthens the city's business and investment climate. The linchpin transportation investment for this area is a multimodal underground railway station which together with the cross-city tunnel will form the heart of the planned High Speed Railway system "Y" V300 serving Warsaw-Łódź-Wrocław/Poznań in Poland – one part of the railway route Rail Baltica which is planned to connect Germany, Poland and the Baltic states. The new transport station will form a hub where central road, railway and airway corridors converge. The train line between Łódź and Warsaw is being modernised with an anticipated 70-minute connection between the two cities.

These developments together with the existing and planned sections of the country's main east-west and north-south highways (A1 and A2) and local expressways (S8 and S14) are opening up new areas for investment. It is anticipated that distribution centres for large corporations and transport and logistics companies will be expanded and new developments will arise. The railway station completes the Władysław Reymont International Airport, which is the regional airport servicing the agglomeration and the *voivodeship* and serves as a back-up airport for Warsaw. In 2013, an express (15-day), weekly rail connection between Łódź's Olechow station and Chengdu in Western China was launched. The freight route offers an alternative to shipping containers with a capacity of 41 containers and travels through Belarus, the Russian Federation and Kazakhstan to the People's Republic of China (hereafter "China"). This development, along with other transportation connections, is leading to an increasing number of logistics warehouses and support services in and around Łódź. Major items for export to China include pharmaceuticals and unique food stuffs.

The greatest pressures for development in Łódź form at the urban-rural fringes of the city where there is demand for single-family homes and property values tend to be higher.[7] Most new multi-family housing developments are concentrated in the eastern fringes of the city.[8] Land outside of the city is cheaper to purchase and there is a preference for single family home ownership over that of other forms of housing (multiunit, attached). Further, incentives such as subsidies for first-time home buyers may further generate housing demand. City planners in Łódź are trying to tackle growing suburbanisation and urban sprawl by searching for suitable areas within the city that could be used for single-family home development – a solution that may require land expropriation, which is presently rarely used in Poland.

Box 2.1. **How's life in Lódzkie region?**

The OECD's Regional Well-Being indicators offer a comparative assessment across 11 dimensions of well-being for 30 countries. Regional well-being indicators for Lódzkie region exhibit strengths in education and jobs. Across the 11 indicators, the Lódzkie region is comparable to the regions of: Northwest (Check Republic), West Slovakia, Southern Great Plain (Hungary) and Antofagasta (Chile).

Figure 2.8. **Lódzkie region well-being indicators**

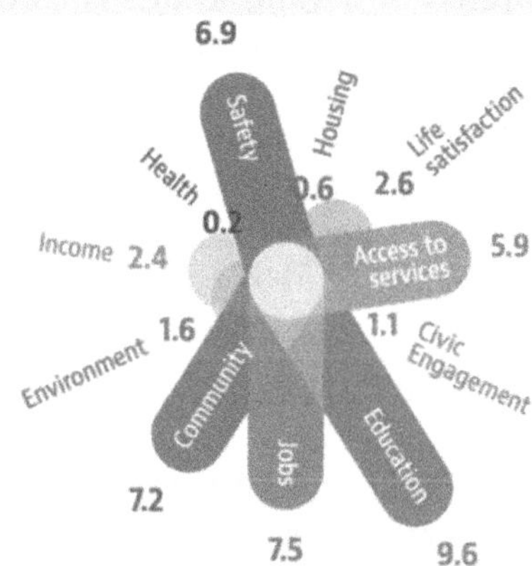

The Lódzkie region ranks high in education; it is among the top 11% of all OECD regions in this indicator. This is measured by the share of the labour force with at least a secondary education, which in the Lódzkie region is 91.9%. The region also fares well in jobs, ranking among the top 41% as measured by the area's employment and unemployment rates (74.2% and 8.9% respectively).

However, the region is less competitive in some other areas. The Lódzkie region ranks among the bottom 5% of all OECD regions in the indicator for health. The region's mortality rate is relatively high at 11.1 deaths per 1 000 people and life expectancy stands at 74.5 years. The region ranks among the bottom 8% of OECD regions for the environment. This indicator is measured by the average level of $PM_{2.5}$ experienced by the population, which in the Lódzkie region stands at 17.5 µg/m³. Civic engagement is among the bottom 11% of all OECD regions with a voter turnout of 51.6% in the Lódzkie region.

The OECD's work on regional well-being uses specific indicators that are proxies for the broader concepts of environment, education and so on. It is recognised that there are many ways to depict well-being. The OECD's work in this area is specifically structured to facilitate comparative analysis between regions.

Source: OECD (2016). "Regional well-being indictors, Lódzkie region", www.oecdregionalwellbeing.org/PL11.html.

The great pressures for land protection include the areas of Landscape Park on Łódź's Hill as well as the Łagiewnicki forest and the river valleys of Jasień, Ner, Sokołówka. Other important areas for land-use protection are Brus (a decommissioned military greenspace), the historical rural layout of Nowosolna, Stoki (semi-urban), Stare Złotno and Mileszki. The historic urban core is also a protected area spanning the central area of the city with blocks of pre-war tenement buildings along with factory complexes, parks and gardens. Łódź is in the midst of revitalising its urban core and seeks to protect its heritage while at the same time permitting new investments. This area is now recognised as an historical monument, which is Poland's highest conservation rating. The historic urban core covers a total of 1 400 hectares and is home to 21% of the population of the city.

Planning tools: Study, plans and decisions

As has been described in Chapter 1, the city of Łódź has three main land-use planning tools: the spatial study, local spatial development plans and finally, planning decisions for areas that are not presently covered by a valid local spatial development plan. In Łódź, only 10.62% of the territory is covered by a valid local land-use plan (as of September 2015). The valid plans are distributed mostly outside of the central city; a few strategic areas, such as the New Centre of Łódź, have a valid development plan. This section describes the goals and objectives of the spatial study and land-use plans, followed by an elaboration on the planning decision mechanism.

Łódź's spatial study

The City Planning Office (est. 2005) is responsible for the production of the spatial study and local spatial plans. This unit is funded through the city budget but is an administratively separate structure from that of the city administration – it is structured independently because it also offers services to the private sector. A body called the Department of Architecture and Development is responsible for delivering planning decisions and permissions (Figure 2.9). This includes the City Architect's Office which works for the executive to provide guidelines, directions and recommendations (Figure 2.10).

Figure 2.9. **City of Łódź organisational chart**

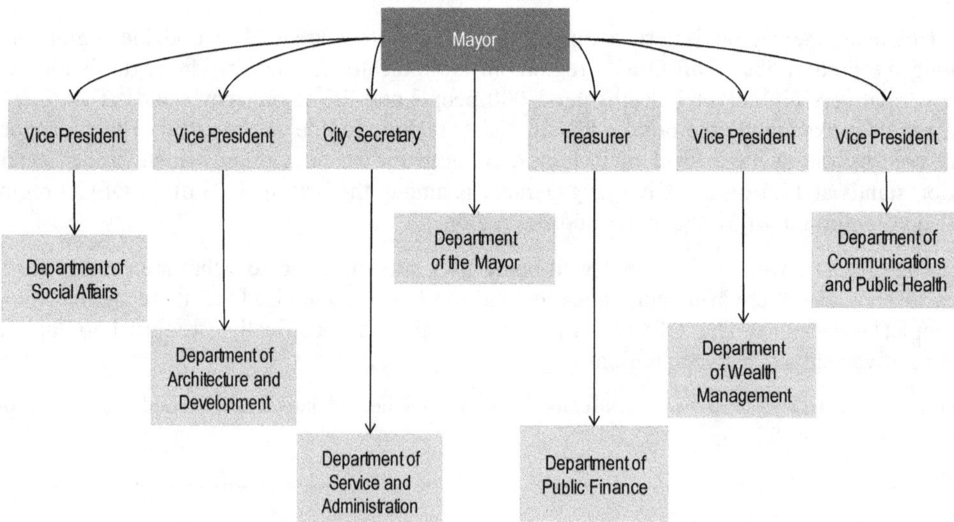

Source: Regulamin Organizacyjny urzędu Miasta Łodzi, Załącznik do zarządzenia Nr 1964/VI/12, Prezydenta Miasta Łodzi z dnia 21 marca 2012 r, http://bip.uml.lodz.pl/_plik.php?id=30546.

Figure 2.10. **Department of Architecture and Development**

Department of Architecture and Development	Roles and responsibilities:
Office of the City Architect	Spatial planning: the development of spatial policy of the city, the schedule of preparing development plans, requesting changes to the local spatial development plan of the city, and theories of urban planning of the city and its monitoring.
Office of Conservation and Monuments	Care and register of monuments and conservation.
City Strategy Office	Monitoring strategies, socio-economic programmes and projects implemented by the city; support in obtaining financial resources from European funds for strategic investment projects; support for integrated territorial investment and ensuring the financing of the Strategy of the Łódź metropolitan area.
Office of Revitalisation and Development	Social housing and local regeneration programme.
Project Management Office	Management and implementation of the New Centre of Łódź programme, International Exhibition EXPO 2022.
Department of Urban Planning and Architecture	Decisions on zoning and land development, building regulations, permits for the investment road district and municipal and decision on the permit to use local roads.

Source: Regulamin Organizacyjny urzędu Miasta Łodzi, Załącznik do zarządzenia Nr 1964/VI/12, Prezydenta Miasta Łodzi z dnia 21 marca 2012 r, http://bip.uml.lodz.pl/_plik.php?id=30546.

Łódź's spatial study ("Study of the conditions and directions of spatial development") outlines the municipality's main planning objectives.[9] The study covers the whole area of the municipality at a scale factor of 1:10 000. Its primary purpose is to guide the city's sustainable development over the medium to long term – encompassing economic/fiscal, environmental and social sustainability. The study gathers all spatial plans (land use, transportation, heritage protection) for the city and acts as an internal management framework study to guide practice. It is not a local by-law, but it is binding for the city to complete the study in advance of the preparation of the local spatial development plans. The study can include measurable objectives. By law, the study's relevance and validity are subject to a review by the municipal executive once per local council tenure. The current spatial study was adopted by the Łódź City Council on 27 October 2010.

The spatial study is prepared by the local government executive, adopted by the city council, and the legality of the procedure is subsequently checked and supervised by the *voivode*. This process is similar to that of the adoption of local spatial development plans. The municipal executive initiates the planning procedure (the resolution to start a procedure must be adopted by the council); residents are notified about the possibility to submit proposals to inform its development and other key institutions/departments are invited submit observations on the plan. The draft document and the environmental impact assessment are prepared and submitted proposals are either accepted or rejected. The plan is then subject to review by the local architectural and planning commission (an independent review body) and subsequently sent for observations and approvals by the external institutions that are entitled, by law, to review the draft document. After the necessary changes, the document is submitted for public presentation and is open for public comments and observations, which may be accepted or rejected. Finally, the document is submitted for approval by the council. This process generally takes a minimum of two years to complete. After being adopted by the local government, the *voivode* supervises its compliance with the law and finally publishes it in the official gazette of the province.

The study discusses all major topics relating to spatial planning within the city, including: 1) settlement structure, creation of the structure of the public spaces, the needs and opportunities for the spatial development; 2) the natural environment and its protection, areas of rural and woodland production; 3) quality of life and living conditions, safety and security (including floods); 4) cultural heritage protection and the management of the urban landscape; 5) areas for urban regeneration; 6) areas in need of preparation of the local development area plan, including the area of the land readjustment and location of the large retail outlets; 7) directions for the development of transportation and technical infrastructure. This includes general city-wide land-use regulations, general zoning and permitted land uses. The plan does not include financial incentives for building development, but it can indicate the permitted land use that can be enforced in the local spatial plans.

It can include recommendations and limitations for development that will be transferred to the local spatial development plans. It does not present comments on the types of buildings that are permitted; however, the development of large-scale retail units is permitted only if the area for their location is designated in the study (it is a prerequisite). The detailed parameters of permitted development, by law, need to be specified in the study, but are legally binding only for local spatial development plans. The study describes the major aims and objectives for environmental protection, but the application and enforcement of detailed environmental regulations falls to environmental law.

The study describes the transportation system – e.g. local roads and transportation corridors, connection with external roads infrastructure, public transport networks, location of the transportation stations and interchanges, car parking standards to be enforced at the level of local spatial development plans and planning permissions. However, the actual management of the public transportation systems falls to other plans (i.e. public transportation plan).

Łódź's spatial development study divides the city into three main zones: 1) the historic urban core; 2) areas of contemporary development; 3) housing and industrial estates, suburbs and non-urbanised areas. Each area has a set of objectives associated with its development (as per the spatial development strategy for the city).

- The main objective for the historic urban core is to preserve as many buildings as possible while maintaining their historic character. Any new structures built in this area are expected to complement the surrounding urban structure. The goals for this area are to create a compact, classic city, while offering good living conditions (i.e. investment in public spaces) and promoting a variety of small businesses (various sizes, functions and standards), mixed with residential function, and even with non-intrusive, "artisanal" production.
- The spatial strategy for the second area (contemporary core development) seeks urban infilling while respecting the urban structure of the city (street and square frontages) and valuable green areas. This includes clear divisions between public and private space; complete frontages; proper care for historic buildings and

complexes; height discipline (frontage up to 25 m, block interior up to 31 m); a decrease in building density if it improves other features (e.g. greenspace).

- The main objective of the third zone (housing and industrial estates, suburbs, non-urbanised areas) is to reduce urban sprawl. Strategies for this zone include: putting a stop to the further growth of single- and multi-family housing in order to protect their advantage of "spatial openness"; prohibiting the development of non-urbanised areas; ensuring that investments are only made where there is infrastructure; locating industrial areas, warehouses, manufacturing facilities and technology parks along main communication routes (connecting the centre with the motorway ring around Łódź). Intensification of currently developed areas is encouraged. Greenbelts are recommended in the case of sensitive investments involving an adverse impact on residents. Therefore, as a general objective, the city's spatial study advocates more compact development and the preservation of its historic structures and greenspaces.

Table 2.2. **Spatial development strategy**

Zone	Main development objectives	Hectares	Surface area of city	Percentage of the population residing in the area
1) Historic urban core	Compact, preservation of historic character, mixed commercial residential	1 400	4.7%	21%
2) Contemporary core development	Urban infilling, protection of green spaces, height discipline.	4 403	14.9%	36%
3) Housing and industrial estates, suburbs, non-urbanised areas	Protect spatial openness, locate industrial areas, warehouses, manufacturing facilities and technology parks and other developments where there is existing access to transport and communications infrastructure	2 3704	80.3%	43%

Source: New Centre of Łódź (2015), "100 hectares in the heart of the city", http://www.ncl.uml.lodz.pl/sites/default/files/NCL%20Folder%20A4%20PL%2025_11_0.pdf.

Local spatial development plans

As the main legally binding ordinances, local spatial developments plans (*Miejscowe plany zagospodarowania przestrzennego*) shape future land development in the city. They provide detailed descriptions of the permitted land use, the scale of developments, rules and regulations for heritage protection (especially in relation to buildings in the local authority registry of protected structures for which the plan is the main tool for legal protection), local infrastructure regulations, land readjustment rules and procedures, and land parcellation. The extent of these plans can vary – from one parcel of approximately 4-37 hectares in the city centre to much larger parts of the city in the case of suburban areas (large-scale plans for approximately 680 ha in the suburban areas). Small-scale and detailed regulatory plans may be drawn at a scale of 1:1 000 or be as detailed as 1:500 for inner city areas. As a regulatory land-use by-law, a local development plan does not contain measurable indicators or objectives. The City Planning Office is responsible for the production of the local plans.

The procedure for the adoption of local spatial development plans follows those outlined in the previous section for spatial studies with two majors exceptions: 1) the timeframe for planning review and commentary differs; 2) most importantly, local spatial development plans become binding ordinances – they are acts of local law published in the regional gazette. Plans can be updated or changed as the municipality sees fit. The timeframe for the development and adoption of a land-use plan can vary from a few months to a few years in the case of very complex projects that may require lengthy consultation and review processes.

Applications for new developments must be compliant with the rules and regulations outlined in the local spatial development plan, which is legally binding for the land owners and local municipality. This includes descriptions of the borders of zoned lands, building lines, heights, maximum and minimum floor area ratio indicators, percentage of the required open space, number and location of the parking spaces.

Local plans need to include legally binding forms of environmental protection that may impact on the permitted land use of the particular development areas and include environmental impact assessment procedures. The plans can also be used to secure public right-of-ways. Should the local authority decide to zone the land for public use, it is obliged to purchase the land from the public owner once the plan has been approved. The list of public uses is specified in the Property Management Act.

Local spatial development plans contain limited information on transportation planning – they detail land-use regulation (in terms of the selection of the road corridors), but as a tool have limited ability to detail road design and traffic organisation (including traffic calming measures). A current law (the Act of 10 April 2003 on the extraordinary rules on preparation and development of national roads) allows for the use of compulsory purchase of land and tracing of public roads independently of local development plans based on the special procedure of Permission for the Procurement of a Road Development (*Zezwolenie na Realizację Inwestycji Drogowej*).

Like many cities in Poland, Łódź overly relies on the planning decision process to approve new or changed lands, developments and buildings (discussed in the following section) due to the low plan coverage. The potential for litigation by citizens (outlined in Article 34 of the Spatial Planning and Development Act) presents a particular encumbrance to the adoption of new plans. This stipulation is indefinite – it is not limited to a particular timeframe. The potential of affected individuals to seek compensation for decreases in property values due to planning decisions also impacts the planning environment. There are plans to increase plan coverage in Łódź; however, this takes a considerable amount of time. Low plan coverage matters as an overall issue, but it is particularly important in areas that are experiencing rapid growth – such as suburban and peri-urban areas.

The planning decision mechanism

In contrast to local spatial plans, planning decisions act as a document for a particular development. Therefore, the scale is that of an individual (site-specific) consideration and not of a neighbourhood as a whole. Hence the common criticism that planning by "decision" leads to a fragmented system that detracts from overarching spatial strategies. Furthermore, authorities have very limited possibilities to reject applications for planning decisions. Thus, even applications for developments that conflict with the spatial strategy of Łódź are frequently approved through planning decisions. There is very limited management of spatial growth when there is reliance on the planning decision mechanism.

Box 2.2. Building permit application

Łódź has one of the shortest processing periods for the issuance of building permits in Poland (World Bank, 2015: 4). Building approvals start with a local plan or a planning decision in the case of its absence. In the case of a valid local plan, there is a need for the proponent to submit an architectural design for the building and apply for a building permit. In cases where there is no local plan, proponents must submit a completed application and, upon completion of this procedural requirement a planning decision will be given and a permit issued. The major difference between the decisions and the local plan is the narrow scope for planning decision; for plans there is opportunity for broader public debate on a project.

New buildings need to be complaint with both building codes and planning regulations. If the documentation is valid, a building permit can be issued in as little as 65 days. The major difference between commercial and residential buildings lies in the additional permits required to lodge the application. Commercial activity may be subject to additional verification, for example due to requirements to submit an environmental impact assessment.

The parameters of the planned building (development) are determined based on the parameters existing in the analysed area, including: the location of the planned investment in relation to the existing buildings (existing conditions of the area), the width and the height of the front elevation, floor to area of land ratio, geometry of the roof. In order to get the decision on land development conditions, one should file an appropriate application. In accordance with Article 52 Section 2, building applications should:

1. Define the boundaries of the area covered by the proposal, presented on a copy of the basic map or, in the absence thereof, the copy of the cadastral map, admitted to the state geodetic and cartographic, covering the area to which it relates, and the area in which this investment will be affected, in a scale of 1:500 or 1:1 000 and, in relation to the line investments (construction of roads, infrastructure networks) also in the scale of 1:2 000.
2. Define the characteristics of investment, including: 1) the amount of water consumption, energy and the method of sewage disposal and treatment, as well as other needs in the field of technical infrastructure, where appropriate, the method of waste disposal; 2) the planned manner of the land development and characteristics of the building and land development, including the purpose and size of the proposed buildings and the land area subject to transformation, presented in a descriptive and graphic form; 3) the specific technical parameters of investment and data characterising its impact on the environment.

Source: City of Łódź (2015), Ustalanie w drodze decyzji lokalizacji inwestycji celu publicznego i warunków zabudowy, http://bip.uml.lodz.pl/index.php?str=16&id=775.

Planning decisions are granted through prescribed legal steps: a nearby plot needs to be developed in a manner similar to the one being proposed; the land must be accessible from a public road; existing infrastructure should be sufficient; there should be no change of land use required and the development should comply with other specific regulations where applicable (e.g. environmental law) (see Table 2.3 for a comparison of the development approval process for plans versus decisions). Where these conditions are met, the development is approved. There is no check for aesthetic judgements. Table 2.3 outlines the considerations for the issuing of a development permit in both instances where there is a valid local spatial plan and where there is none (planning decisions). In the case of a planning decision, the relevant local authorities review the planning conditions (the legal facts regarding the land and its proposed development). The application of the procedure can be ambivalent – e.g. the term "adjacent" is not clearly understood and role of "good neighbourhood" criteria is unclear (where investments should be in compliance with the character of the neighbourhood). Discretionary powers can inform a planning decision on the basis of the urban analysis.

Table 2.3. **Comparison of the development approval process**

Local development plans versus planning decisions

Application requirements where there is a valid local spatial development plan	Application requirements where there is no valid local spatial development plan – planning decision
– Copy of the main plan (1:500 or 1:1 000) or, if there is no such plan, a copy of the cadastral map showing the ownership and value of plots adjacent to the one to which the application refers. – Estimates of the water and energy consumption and the method of sewage disposal during the construction work, and other needs relating to public infrastructure, and if necessary, the method of waste neutralisation. – Description of the planned method of land development and characteristic planning features, including the function and size of the designed buildings and facilities presented in a graphical and descriptive form. – Specification of technical parameters of the investment and information describing its environmental impact.	– At least one nearby plot, accessible from the same public road, is developed in a manner allowing determination of requirements for the planned investment as regards the continuation of: land development, use purposes, parameters, features and ratios, dimensions and architectural form of the buildings and facilities, building line, degree of land exploitation. – The land must be accessible from a public road. – The existing or designed infrastructure is sufficient for the planned investment. – No consent should be needed for a change of purpose of agricultural or forest lands to non-agricultural or non-forest, or such consent had already been issued in relation to the land but on the basis of local master plans that have already expired. – The decision is compliant with specific regulations (such as the Environmental Law, the Monument Protection Law).

Source: Polish Information and Foreign Investment Agency (2015), "Construction process", www.paiz.gov.pl/polish_law/construction_process.

Planning decisions require that any parties directly affected by the decision be informed of the proposed development. NGOs that may wish to be involved need to apply to be a part of the process. In general, public engagement with the planning decisions process is much more limited than that for area plans – it is easier for planning decisions to escape community debate and discussion. Property owners who may be affected by a planned development can appeal the decision to allow it. There is no clause for residents who may abuse the appeals system; 7%-8% of all planning decisions are appealed and a little over half of appeals are successful. Decisions are typically appealed on the basis of procedural error, wrong application of law or wrong proceedings.

If the planning conditions meet the requirements, a planning decision will be issued. A refusal may be issued only if the intended use of land infringes upon public interest that is protected by law or upon a third party's interest. A decision can become invalid, however, in instances where another applicant is granted a building permit, or a new local plan is adopted which changes the conditions for development.

While the above descriptions of the development process detail the procedure, the process of obtaining a development permit in practice involves a fair amount of upfront communication with city officials. Typically, one year before applying for a construction permit, an investor will ask the city to make a due diligence report of the real estate in order to determine: that it has access to a public road; whether it is entered into the register of cultural or heritage zones; and whether it is protected by environmental provisions. This is done in order to ensure the investor is aware of the requirements of the plot. The process requires approval from a minimum of 20 authorities. From the perspective of the developer, the process can last one to two years, or for a large-scale investment, two to four years. Investors generally try and maintain good contact with the city because it speeds up the process. In the case of heritage buildings, there can be some negotiation between the developer and the heritage planner.

Table 2.4. **Economic right in the land development process, Poland**

Type of cost	Description
The cost of drawing up a local detailed plan	The cost to draw up the local plan is covered in general from the municipality's budget. Only the cost of drawing up or changing the local plan as a result of the allocation of public investment of national, regional or county importance is covered respectively by the state budget, the region's budget or the county's budget. The private, commercial developer has neither the right to organise/produce nor to finance plans.
Infrastructure costs	System of planning charges – a special one-time fee and betterment charges. If, in connection to the enactment of a local plan or its amendment, the value of the property has increased, and the owner or perpetual user sells the property, the municipal administrator gets a one-off fee, as set out in the local plan. This one-off fee is set out in relation to the percentage increase in the value of the property; it cannot be higher than 30%. The fee is charged in cases when the owner sells the real estate within five years from the date when the local plan or its revision came into force. Betterment charges are levied after the creation of conditions for connecting the property to individual devices of the technical infrastructure or conditions for the use of built roads. The construction of technical infrastructure is understood as the building of roads and underground, on ground or above ground pipes or infrastructural equipment for water, sewage, heating, electrical, gas and telecommunications. The betterment charges depend on the increase in land value caused by the construction of technical infrastructure facilities. The value of betterment charges shall not be higher than 50% of the value of the difference between the value of the land before and after the technical infrastructure facilities are built.
Transfer of street and public road areas to the municipality	The land owner must transfer to the local authority those parcels that have been separated for streets, and in return should receive compensation in cash or in the form of land. However, most municipalities do not have funds to pay the compensation.
Compensation to land owners for land-use restrictions included in the local plans	Compensation is paid in connection to the enactment of a local plan or its amendment. However, most municipalities do not have funds to pay the compensation, which seriously hinders planning activities.
The right to development gain/increase in land value	Passive land policy of the municipality. Expropriation allowed in the areas covered by the local plans which are designated in the plan for public purposes, therefore an increase in land value due to planning belongs to the private land owner in expropriation process.

Source: Havel, M.B. (2014), "Delineation of property rights as institutional foundations for urban land markets in transition", http://dx.doi.org/10.1016/j.landusepol.2014.01.004.

Integrated spatial planning

In Łódź, the aforementioned planning tools – study, local spatial development plans and planning decisions – influence and shape the urban environment. However, so do various private and public strategies and investments, such as the city's integrated development strategy, major infrastructure investments, the creation of special economic zones, and a host of social and economic development programmes and projects.

Integrated planning has emerged as a new spatial planning orthodoxy (Vigar, 2009). Such an agenda can be described as having four related dimensions: the (co)alignment of strategies and policies; policy reframing; the connection between policies and actions; and co-operation among actors (Healey, 2006). Experience in OECD countries shows that integrated planning favours socially inclusive and environmentally sustainable territorial development that can significantly contribute to economic growth (OECD, 2013). Łódź's long-term development strategy (Integrated Development Strategy for Łódź 2020+) plays a role in this regard.[10,11] It describes the major challenges facing the city and outlines recommended policy actions; it is a Resolution of Council that was adopted in 2012 (City of Łódź, 2012). It is in effect a non-binding document that guides the city's development and communicates expectations to citizens. The strategy is oriented around three pillars, of which "space and the environment" form one element.[12] The strategic objectives related to this pillar are the regeneration of the city centre, cohesive development that preserves greenspace, the development of sustainable transportation options, and increased safety and security. This strategy is prepared by the City Strategy Bureau along with input from other departments and local non-governmental institutions. The strategy includes monitoring indicators and is linked to multiannual financial plans.

EU funds have been used to finance a large number of infrastructure investments, including the development of major roads, housing revitalisation, sewage and water main construction and upgrades. This infrastructure has the potential to increase private investment to the region and create employment. However, it is important that these investments are linked to broader spatial and economic strategies for the region and incorporate demographic forecasts.

The revitalisation of the historic city centre is the largest and most important project to date – it is co-financed with EU and city funds. It is the largest project of this kind in Poland, with 100 hectares to be developed. The regeneration project is combined with initiatives to support low-income neighbourhoods, including employment and training schemes. Over PLN 1 billion of EU funds have been attracted to Łódz to date – including the funds gained throughout Poland's EU accession. There is a strategic projects department financed by the European Union with a list of projects that will be financed with EU funds. The city is also preparing a low-emission economic plan required for applications to European structural and investment funds and has developed a list of primary and secondary projects.

Transportation master plans are on the level of general plans – they show the general corridors but not the detail. The general transportation strategy that has been prepared for Łódź has not yet been prescribed in law; it is anticipated that the two plans will merge in 2016.

There are silos within the city's administration that affect land acquisition, management and planning. Different units within the city's administration do not always co-ordinate their land acquisitions. For example, the Department of Finance may sell land to provide revenue for the city – land which may also have some strategic value for public development. Units within the city administration may thus work at cross purposes and have information asymmetries.

Special economic zones

Special economic zones (SEZ) in Poland were first created in the 1990s – they are an administratively separate part of Polish territory allocated to run businesses on preferential terms.[13] In Łódź, the SEZs grant investors state aid of up to 55% of investment costs through a combination of personal and corporate income tax exemptions. They were first created as a regional economic policy to reduce structural unemployment, manage post-industrial properties and infrastructure, and attract foreign investors. Since that time they have proliferated – there are 14 SEZs today. Each of the 14 zones are governed by a management board which helps investors purchase and develop land.[14]

The Łódź SEZ was established in 1997 and under current legislation will continue to exist until 2020. It occupies an area of 1 302 hectares across 3 regions: Łódź, Masovia and Greater Poland and includes 45 subzones. To date it is reported that 272 permits have been granted and employment for 29 000 individuals has been created (Polish Information and Foreign Investment Agency, 2015). The term "zone", however, is misleading. A single zone consists of many unconnected parcels of land with access to utilities and roads/transport and/or warehouses and office spaces that are owned by a city or commune (in most cases). Many of these are listed as greenfield sites (as opposed to brownfield sites, which the NSDC advocates should be developed in advance of any greenfield sites).

The 2010 OECD *Economic Survey of Poland* questioned the efficiency of the SEZ mechanism (OECD, 2010). In particular, it questioned the induced distortions between firms inside and outside the zones, and the amount of public aid involved, especially as competition among governments might result in overbidding for investment projects. The 2010 review further questioned whether the SEZ resources might be better used to improve the overall investment climate. The report advocates transforming the SEZ approach into a policy focused instead on developing economic clusters based on innovation and linked to local firms. Łódź's SEZ shows scattered developments that, though coherently linked to infrastructure, are not coherently linked to one another.

The New Centre of Łódź

The city is embarking on a large-scale urban regeneration programme which includes housing and commercial (re)developments, new transportation infrastructure – most importantly, a high-speed rail link and Łódź Fabryczna railway station. The programme was first adopted by the Municipal Council in 2007. It targets 100 hectares in the centre of the city and encompasses over 50 projects at a total cost of PLN 5 billion (New Centre of Łódź, 2015). This regeneration plan builds on past successes – for example, the city has supported building renovation and has created an impressive pedestrian area along its historical high street (ul. Piotrkowska). The redevelopment involves multiple stakeholders: ministries, railway companies, departments of the City Office of Łódź, commercial law companies, the organisational units of the City Office of Łódź, the Marshal's Office, the Łódź Voivodeship Office, enterprises, foundations and other organisations.

The urban regeneration programme has adopted a corporate management model; its Management Board is an organisational unit of the City of Łódź and has the status of a budgetary entity. It is supervised by the Mayor of the city of Łódź. Since its initiation, the New Centre of Łódź programme has been "public" to a limited extent. The city has assumed the classical role of "a night watchman" and has retained control over zoning, ownership and the overarching development strategy. Three local spatial development plans are in the process of being developed for the New Centre of Łódź. All historic buildings will be kept and integrated with existing or newly developed components (tenement buildings, the Łódź Fabryczna railway station, EC1, the Moniuszki Park with the Orthodox Church, the University of Łódź Campus, etc.).

This programme is part of broader spatial development goals within the city to increase urban density within the urban core. The urban core is envisaged as an area of mixed land uses and multi-modal transportation. For this scale and scope of development to succeed, the space will need to meet the needs of both residents and businesses and balance the interests of density and compact urban form with a liveable scale, green spaces and public amenities. While development efforts are concentred on the New Centre of Łódź, this will undoubtedly affect the areas surrounding it; up-to-date local spatial development plan coverage should be a priority for these adjoining areas.

Fiscal tools and incentives

In Poland there are few available fiscal instruments (taxes and fees) at the local level. The most important among these is property taxes, which are not based on property value but on land and building area/size and differ according to types of usage (e.g. residential, commercial).[15] The Minister of Finance announces yearly upper limits for property taxation which then inform local government resolutions that determine local rates. Only one element of the Polish property tax system is based on a value – the tax on construction structures used for an economic activity, which is based on book value.

In 2013, approximately 68% of Łódź's budget was composed of own-source revenues (Statistical Office in Łódź, 2014b). Of these, the local government's share in personal income taxes out of total own-source revenues stood at 30%; the share of corporate income taxes out of total own-source revenues stood at 2.7%. Out of all taxes levied directly by the local government, the largest share is that of the property tax, which in 2013 composed approximately 11% of all own-source revenues.

Łódź uses limited land-use value-capture mechanisms through non-recurrent taxes. By law the city can employ a planning levy on land that increased its value due to the preparation of the local spatial development plans and can also charge a betterment levy. By law the city can ask a developer to improve elements of road infrastructure where a development will have an impact on the road network. The municipality can also increase the value of its own land via preparation of the local spatial development plans and sell the property (as a short-term gain). Land-use value-capture through recurrent taxation and tax-based schemes are also used. The municipality uses land-value taxation, property lease and assessments on the "right of perpetual usufruct" (see Box 2.3 for a description of perpetual usufruct). The municipality uses the emission of obligations and credits to cover the costs of infrastructure as a city-wide tax increment financing scheme. Presently, the municipality does not use tax increment financing schemes (at least not directly related to particular plots), air rights charges or negotiated exactions.

Łódź does not have an official policy on the use of land-use value-capture mechanisms; however, their usage is described in local tax ordinances, in the public budget (in case of the financial mechanisms) and in the long-term budgeting plan (*Wieloletni Plan Finansowy*). Laws on local taxation and the Spatial Planning and Development Act of 2003 define precisely how and what assessments can be levied on a land owner; this places limits on the ways that municipalities can use assessments. In the case of tax revenue-based financial mechanisms, the other limiting factor is budgetary discipline that limits municipalities' ability to borrow. At present, not all of the available fiscal instruments (taxes and fees) are being used in Łódź; there is no spa fee (because it is not relevant, and the dog fee is not collected because of high administration costs).

Local spatial development plans account for the fiscal impacts of changing land use in Łódź through the requirements of the Spatial Planning and Development Act 2003; the statement of the financial impact of the local development plan must be prepared and submitted for review before the plan is accepted. The statement details the projected gains (through tax increases, assessments) and losses (due to infrastructural costs, compulsory purchase orders, etc.). The financial analysis at the level of the spatial study has so far been voluntary. In Łódź, initial assessments have been made in order to conduct basic estimations on the impacts of zoning of new land on the cost of new infrastructure.

It bears mentioning that in 2011 the city adopted a resolution to conduct fiscal forecasting exercises, the most recent of which analyses the period from 2016-40 (City of Łódź, 2011). This is an important tool to understand both how revenues and expenditures may change over time, as well as the depreciation of fixed assets. This forecasting exercise includes an element of citizen engagement wherein citizens have the chance to forward project proposals to inform city expenditures (Miasta Łodzi, 2015). The forecasts are based on a range of assumptions – from the depreciation of capital assets to the size of the population, wherein its accuracy is diminished the further out the timeframe considered. In general terms, the total anticipated revenue of the city shows a strong increase over time, with income tax contributions being a major contributor. The contribution of property tax to total taxes and fees remains constant throughout the scenario at approximately 48%. Budget overruns (total revenue less total expenditure) show a sharp increasing trend to the year 2025 and slight declines thereafter.

Box 2.3. The Polish perpetual usufruct system

Poland's unique perpetual usufruct system, while gradually being phased out, affects how national and local governments manage the residential properties they own. Generally, usufruct is a type of property right recognised mostly by civil law systems, and in strict legal terms is defined by "the right of use and enjoyment, for a certain time, of property owned by another as one's own, subject to the obligation of preserving its substance". In Poland, perpetual usufruct is a form of public leasehold contract that grants the lessee broader property rights than the above definition, and is regarded as falling between a long-term leasehold and full ownership (Dale-Johnson and Brzeski, 2001). Polish cities have considerable land holdings held under perpetual usufruct. Some of the perpetual usufruct land is in the historic city centres or nearby; the rest is on the outskirts of cities where major housing projects were built during communist times.

Usufructs are both an asset and a liability for municipalities. On the positive side, the usufruct contracts provide an additional avenue for regulating land use and development. Perpetual usufruct ground lease contracts are sometimes used as surrogates for land-use and development controls, although this use may be marginal. The existence of usufructs may facilitate urban revitalisation, as they may permit the government to more easily assemble land parcels into large enough tracts for regeneration investments. However, this advantage is likely to be marginal, since the holders of the usufruct contracts for the buildings all have extensive rights and must each be approached individually. On the negative side, the municipality is responsible for the maintenance costs of the yard – the area not covered by buildings. Municipalities are often unable to keep up with this burden, resulting in a lower level of grounds upkeep than with privately owned buildings.

In view of the general policy favouring privatisation, municipalities (and the central government) have encouraged the conversion of usufruct contracts into private ownership. Some owners do not see the advantage, as it adds little in market price. Where units are privatised, the land also falls under private ownership. Because the dominant mode of housing is multiple-unit buildings, incremental privatisation of units makes the municipality a co-owner with various private owners in a condominium-like legal structure. Maintenance costs are then shared. Since the maintenance of condominium units is notoriously difficult even where all participants are private owners (Alterman, 2010), the combination of private and public housing unit owners in the same building is bound to compromise the maintenance of building quality. Given the burden that perpetual usufruct properties can represent for municipalities, which may outweigh any increased control they may have over these properties, it would seem to be in the municipalities' interest to continue the phasing out of the perpetual usufruct system.

Source: OECD (2011b), *OECD Urban Reviews, Poland 2011*, http://dx.doi.org/10.1787/9789264097834-en.

Functional metropolitan planning and co-operation

Both Poland's national and regional spatial strategies highlight the importance of adopting a functional perspective for regions. The long-term regional strategy identifies poor functional connections, a lack of regional identity and rampant spatial conflicts related to (sub) urbanisation as major problems (Łódź Regional Government, 2006: 34). It identifies a need to change the present settlement network and to increase the role of towns in the functional and spatial management and recommends that the region: strengthen its functional associations with regional and supra-local settlement centres and the Warsaw Metropolitan Area; promote a network model of co-operation between towns; and support the development of inter-regional connections between regional centres, other towns and rural settlements (Łódź Regional Government, 2006: 35). The new Metropolitan Association Act (2015) offers a framework to pursue such functional planning.

At present, some local governments have adopted measures of their own accord. Funding for EU projects offer an impetus in this regard. The bodies responsible for the overall co-ordination of the planning process activities between municipalities in the neighbourhood are the competent authorities to agree on the planning documents. These include primarily: the Governor of the Łódź region (*voivode*), the Marshal of the Łódź region, the Board of the Łódź region, the environmental authorities and other authorities established by law.[16]

The need for a functional approach to spatial planning is further reinforced by the European Union's integrated territorial investments (ITI), which are part of its 2014-2020 Cohesion Policy. The structure of these funds push municipalities to promote projects based on a partnership collaboration model, in order to increase the effectiveness of interventions and the influence of cities that are functionally associated with them.

Łódź's functional urban area is one of the beneficiaries of these funds. In its legal form this involves co-operation and agreements between municipalities and communities across the Łódź metropolitan area in which there are 31 municipalities. This area will receive approximately 16.5% out of total fund allocations for the country (EUR 226 million) (Ministry for Infrastructure and Development, n.d.).

The Association of Łódź Metropolitan Municipalities is presently focused on the urban regeneration process. The Municipal Association has also joined a consortium for public tenders for energy purchases used to purchase energy for building offices and companies. Municipalities also co-ordinate on the SEZ which surrounds Łódź and co-operate in the delivery of social, education and healthcare services and on sewage and water services. Łódź's Water Treatment Plan serves the municipal agglomeration. Łódź's heating system is served by one company and surrounding communes are beginning to be connected to it within a radius of 50 km. This co-operation exists through agreements or associations.

Municipalities, both large and small, compete with one another. Per capita income tax transfers are a major source of local government funding and, as a result, cities and communes compete with one another for population growth. Some local governments have realised that they would be better off co-ordinating with one another and have organised metropolitan associations which link spatial policies – e.g. Gdańsk and Poznan (Box 2.4). However, these tend to be the exception. There are few structural incentives for municipalities to co-ordinate on public investments. Currently there is no legal basis for communes and municipalities to have a common local plan.

Box 2.4. Urban regeneration in Gdańsk

There are a number of similarities between Łódź and Gdańsk, which make it an interesting comparative case for urban regeneration. Like Łódź, the city is experiencing population decline; it too has an historic urban core with 19th century housing as well as numerous former industrial structures; and it also has central areas with enclaves of poverty that are experiencing gentrification. In a review of urban regeneration policies in Gdańsk, Sagan and Grabkowska profile projects in three neighborhoods: Dolne Miasto, Nowy Port and Dolny Wrzeszcz. Regeneration efforts in Gdańsk were first adopted in 2004 and, the authors argue, were created to take advantage of EU funding; the availability of EU funds "opened up new possibilities for financing more holistic approaches to inner-city regeneration…" (Sagan and Grabkowska, 2012: 1 148). The resulting urban regeneration efforts included public consultations and local government partnership with non-governmental organisations, private sector foundations and a wide range of institutions (e.g. churches, schools) to promote social inclusion in tandem with urban regeneration.

However, Sagan and Grabkowska critique the regeneration efforts as being overly focused on physical regeneration with the aim of making the city more attractive to business and tourism. They conclude that, "while top-down projects can be highly effective in promoting physical regeneration, bottom-up processes are of critical significance for social and demographic regeneration" (2012: 1 135). They recommend that urban regeneration efforts employ mixed strategies which invest in physical spaces along with public services to more effectively address social inclusion. Poland's recently adopted Revitalization Act (2015) addresses such critique by defining revitalisation zones according to both their social and physical dimensions.

Source: Sagan, I. and M. Grabkowska (2012), "Urban regeneration in Gdańsk, Poland: Local regimes and tensions between top-down strategies and endogenous renewal", http://dx.doi.org/10.1080/09654313.2012.674347.

From the city's perspective it was also expressed that it is a struggle to think about the metropolitan area – the functional area. City officials expressed a need for more detailed and timely data at the city district level and more data on surrounding communes. This would help to understand the dynamics of suburbanisation and sprawl; better data at the lowest level would enable combined analysis with metropolitan and city-scaled data.[17] A 2014 article analysing population density across Polish cities reiterates the comments made by city staff on the availability of small-scale data. The author, Śleszyński, notes that, "work done to date on population-density profiles – and more broadly on the structure to population configurations within urbanised areas – has been limited by the availability of statistical data for small spatial units" (2014: 73). He further remarks that the 2002 Census data are the most recently available to provide such disaggregation and that, while it was anticipated that the 2011 Census would produce robust small-scale data, a growing chorus of researchers has criticized its validity (2014: 73). It bears noting that the introduction of the EU INSPIRE directive (2007) in Poland on the interoperability of geographic data systems has led to a push for the greater integration of ICT in planning. Another important factor is the steadily growing availability of data hosted by the geoportals of the state agencies and statistical offices.

Public engagement

A basic function of local spatial planning is to negotiate conflict between potentially competing land uses, to balance private and public interests, and to shape future developments. As such, public engagement forms an important part of contemporary planning practices, provides opportunities for individuals to know about proposed plans and comment on them such that their opinions might be incorporated into the decision-making process – this entails a fundamental change from rational policy-making models regarding how policy is formulated, conducted and implemented.

While indicators of social capital and social trust are exceptionally low in Poland – both in comparison to other western countries and among other former communist ones – a culture of public engagement in the planning process in Poland is growing (Lasinska, 2013). By law, there is a prescribed process of public feedback associated with the elaboration of local spatial development plans; residents and other interested parties can lodge proposals and observations. According to the Spatial Planning and Development Act 2003, public participation in the planning process has three aims: 1) to inform the public about the development of new plans or the creation of existing ones; 2) to receive feedback from all actors in the process; 3) to either incorporate or reject the resulting feedback while giving rationales for doing so. There are two steps to every planning procedure. First, the public is provided with the proposed changes and may submit observations. This is a formal process through which observations may be submitted in writing and by email. Next, the plan being presented is open for public comment. Grievances on the resulting planning decisions can be made through the court. The legality of the planning procedure, including public input and engagement, are checked by the *voivode*.

By the letter of the law as set out in the Spatial Planning and Development Act 2003, public engagement on local spatial development plans can be rather limited. There can be significant differences in how open the engagement process is and how meaningfully the public is engaged in decision making. The public participation component may have open or restrictive communication and plans may be presented at different stages of development (with more competitive ones offering less scope to shape outcomes). There is leeway for city planners to shape the engagement process to allow for more or less deliberation depending on their aims. Within the planning literature, a trade-off is often described between the efficiency of getting a plan through and the effectiveness of the outcome. Planning processes which limit the amount of public engagement may be pushed through the system faster but on the other end may experience dissent or litigation due to unresolved conflicts. A 2007 study of land-use development in Poland described community involvement in the spatial planning process as "formal and only protect[ing] legal (as opposed to factual) interests of inhabitants and owners, while failing to encourage municipalities to offer alternative development solutions" (Izdebski, Nelicki and Zachariasz, 2007: 12).

Public engagement processes in spatial planning are increasingly valued in Łódź, but practices can be mixed. The current spatial study was offered as an example of an inadequate public participation process, with poor timing and some open antagonism between residents and planners. As a counter example, the present planning process for the development of the historic urban core was described as a more successful example of meaningful public engagement.[18] It involved the public at an earlier stage of the plan's development and opened the process up to participation on three separate occasions as opposed to one. Public participation in the plan was high; over 200 residents participated and there have been 80 meetings with land owners. As a result of this deliberative process, elements of the plan were modified, such as the addition of a new public space in the centre and the addition of more green space. This engagement process proceeded for a year and a half. The adoption of a more elaborate process of public engagement for this area of the city was seen as highly valuable given its central importance, density and heritage.

Community level advisory bodies may come to play an increasingly important role in focusing citizen engagement. Such bodies have replaced the district structure to some extent; they are small councils composed of community representatives who are compensated on a per diem basis.[19] Presently there are approximately 50 such units. These bodies have very small budgets and tend to have influence on small community investments. They may also raise issues to council and lobby for their areas. Since 2009, a portion of a commune's or municipality's budget has been set aside for local residents to vote on (Solecki Fund). The advisory bodies are involved in this form of participatory budgeting at the local/community level. Łódź is a pioneer in this regard – it is the second-largest city in Poland to undertake a participatory budgeting process. During the last participatory budget, 128 000 people voted (approximately 18% of the population), which is a very high turnout rate.

Łódź has a growing number of NGOs that are engaged in such issues as sustainable transportation, citizen engagement and urban revitalisation. While many of these organisations engage with local government through advocacy, they have also in some instances managed aspects of the engagement process and delivered civic education. It was expressed that many residents were against the new road junction in the centre of the city; in response to this, the Mayor called for an online (non-binding) Internet poll on the issue. The city is learning to work with NGOs and brings them in from time to time as collaborators to support citizen engagement. One of the most prominent examples of this is a local NGO that was brought in to help engage local residents in the participatory budgeting process.

Representatives of Łódź's non-profit sector were critical of the way the city shares information with the broader public and involves them in decision-making processes. The NGO sector tends to engage in the planning process in ad hoc ways – e.g. through the informal competition that was launched for the design of the new central train station. They expressed a desire for more consistent and formalised engagement with stronger communications efforts to inform organisations and individuals of planned investments and developments.

Box 2.5. **Influences from academia: The University of Łódź**

Spatial and land-use planning in Łódź benefits from an active university sector, in particular the Faculty of Geography of the University of Łódź which was established at the end of the Second World War. The connections between the faculty and the planning field are readily apparent: city staff conduct collaborative research projects with faculty members, hold degrees from the school and teach in it as adjuncts.

Urban land-use planning is one of the major research focuses of the faculty (comprising approximately 30% of the faculty's publications). The faculty has engaged in collaborative studies with national and local governments, including the joint preparation of strategies (e.g. development strategies in the towns of Inowrocław and Uniejów), administrative reform (e.g. dividing Łódź into local units, delimitation of the Łódź Voivodship), the development of land-use inventories (e.g. in Aleksandrów, Łódzki), and have been involved in urban revitalisation projects (e.g. Pabianice). Members of the faculty have also provided expert reports on changing administrative borders and co-operation within metropolitan areas and have been involved in the digitisation of geographic information.

Source: Lamprecht M. (2014), "Urban land use planning"; http://dspace.uni.lodz.pl:8080/xmlui/bitstream/handle/11089/5530/Lamprecht_URBAN%20LAND%20USE%20PLANNING.pdf?sequence=1.

Urban-rural linkages

Urban and rural areas are highly interconnected. These linkages take various forms, such as systems of governance (formal and informal institutions), migration and labour market flows, environmental and ecosystem preservation and enhancement, investment and economic transactions, and infrastructure and service provision (OECD, 2013). Public policy shapes urban-regional morphology and infrastructure and service provision – either intentionally or unintentionally.[20] It is important for public policy to focus attention on urban-rural dynamics in order to develop consistent, effective and intentional policies in this regard. There is a growing interest in the planning profession to refocus planning across the whole spectrum of the urban-rural continuum. This often requires creating mechanisms to co-operate with other governments across scales – local, regional and national.

In the Łódź region (*voivodeship*), population projections indicate that, as a whole, the population is expected to decline and that this decline will be much stronger in urban areas than in rural ones. The forecast population trend for rural areas appears relatively flat into the year 2050 (Figure 2.11). While this could change, such a scenario is consistent with the developments surrounding Łódź, where rural areas connected to the city are maintaining or even growing their populations (Brzeziński, 2010).

Such peri-urbanisation places pressures on limited land resources and can create competition for different types of land uses – residential, recreation, industrial, agricultural. In such contexts, land-use planning has an important role to play in balancing diverse interests and demands on urban, suburban, peri-urban and rural landscapes.

Figure 2.11. **Łódz region, rural and urban population projections**

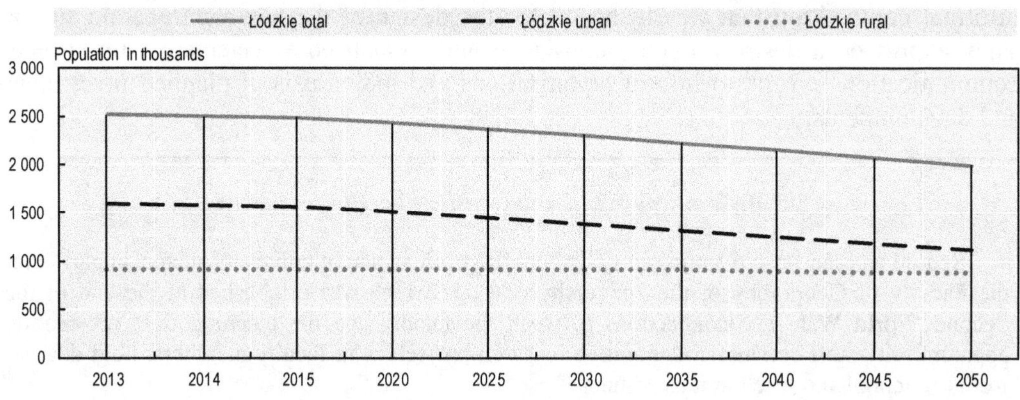

Source: Central Statistical Office of Poland (2014), "Population projection 2014-2050", http://stat.gov.pl/en/topics/population/population-projection/population-projection-2014-2050,2,5.html.

The following two maps further illustrate these dynamics. The city of Łódź is a regional pole; as shown in Figure 2.12, it has by far the largest population in the region, at 706 004 in 2014. This is approximately 28% of the population of the region as a whole. However, at the same time, the city of Łódź is experiencing the greatest population decline while surrounding *powiats* are seeing population increases (Figure 2.13). Between 2006 and 2014, the population of the city of Łódź declined by 7.61%. In contrast, all of the city's surrounding *powiats* saw population increases over that period, by as much as 8.61% in Łódź east and 2.60% in Zgierz, 1.13% in Brzeziny and 0.48% in Pabianice.

Figure 2.12. **Łódź region, population by *powiat*, 2014**

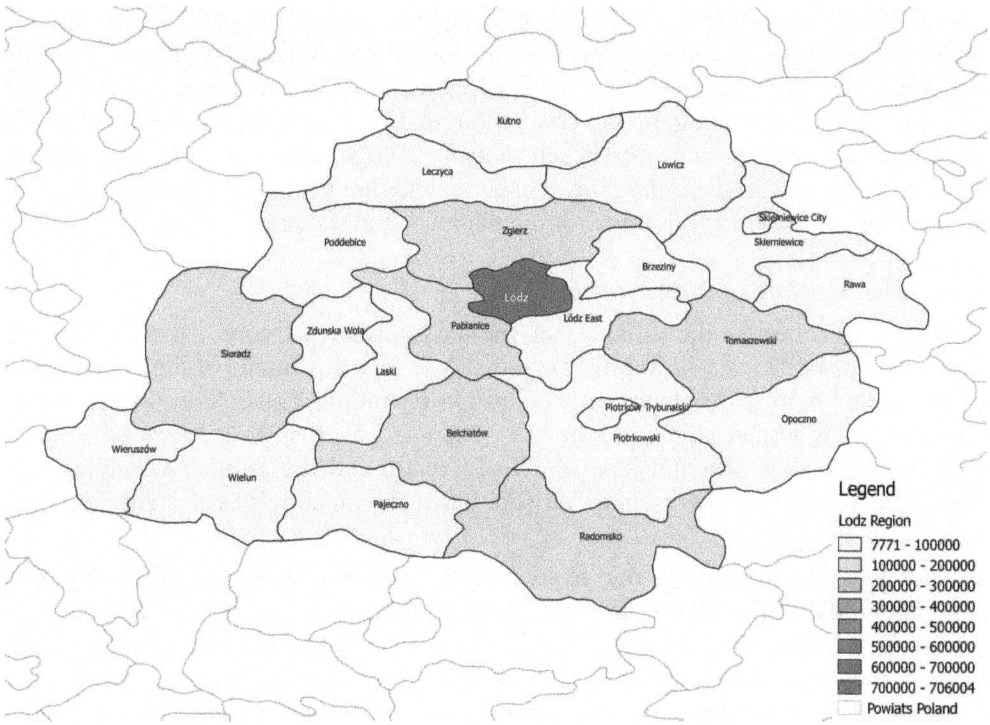

Source: Own elaboration.

Figure 2.13. **Łódź region, population change by *powiat*, 2006-14**

Source: Own elaboration.

Because of these dynamics, urban-rural linkages are extremely important. For instance, many residents from surrounding rural municipalities work or attend school in Łódź proper, use the services of the central city and shop there. Meanwhile, the adjacent rural communes provide food, greenspace and recreation/tourism for urban residents. These issues are explored by examining the case of the rural *gmina* of Nowosolna which borders Łódź's northeast. Nowosolna was chosen as a city to highlight in this report because it is located to the east of Łódz in the *powiat* experiencing the strongest population growth. It is in this sense competing with Łódź for population – and doing so successfully.

The rural commune of Nowosolna

Nowosolna's heart – the village that formerly formed its core – was amalgamated with the city of Łódź in 1989 in order for the city to take advantage of the area's land fill and sand mine, neither of which are presently in operation. Thus, Nowosolna's name is connected to this former structure which it no longer governs. As a result, Nowosolna's identity is unclear; it does not have a defined centre and the municipal administration building sits outside of Nowosolna's jurisdiction at the junction of the eight radial roads that formerly defined it.

Much as Łódź is attractive due to its central location – so too is Nowosolna, which sits in the middle of four districts. But its demographic characteristics differ from that of Łódź: its population is younger and is growing as opposed to the municipality of Łódź, where it is older and shrinking (Table 2.5). Nowosolna has a large working age population and robust local government revenues as a result. Many of the residents commute to Łódź to work. While the commune has many services of its own (schools, a library), its residents may also draw on the services in the city of Łódź.

Unlike Łódź, Nowosolna has full local spatial development plan coverage. There is one local spatial development plan for 95% of the area of the municipality and very detailed plans for the remainder of the areas – for a total of 21 plans (scaled to 1:2 000). The *gmina* first adopted its local spatial development plans in 2001 (two years prior to the adoption of the Spatial Planning and Development Act 2003). When the new law came into force the municipality was able to carry these plans over because they corresponded to the new legislative requirements. The municipality subsequently sped up the process to cover the whole area; in 2003 when the new law came in to effect, only 5% of the *gmina* had plan coverage; subsequently a plan for the remaining 95% of the territory was adopted. It was described that residents had limited awareness of the zoning process at that time and the level of public input into the plan's development was limited. The municipality decided to adopt 20 small plans in order to reduce the potential for the appeals process to hamper their adoption; these plans are mostly for residential permits. In the past, land owners could co-finance the development of a local spatial development plan. This is no longer allowed by law as it creates pressure from investors.

Table 2.5. **Rural *gmina* of Nowosolna, summary statistics, 2013**

Area (km²)	54
Population density (per km²)	84
Total population	4 556
Proportion of population under the age of 18	22%
Proportion of the population ages 18-64	63%
Proportion of the population ages 65 and over	15%

Source: Statistical Office in Łódź (2014b), *Lódzkie Voivodship 2014: Subregions, Powiats, Gminas*, http://lodz.stat.gov.pl/en/publications/statistical-yearbook/lodzkie-voivodship-2014-subregions-powiats-gminas,2,16.html.

Local spatial development plans can act as an instrument of land speculation, particularly in rural areas where they may be used to unlock investment opportunities. For this reason, many rural areas have found it easier to adopt local spatial development plans as they present an opportunity for land owners. In urban areas – particularly urban cores – existing buildings, construction permits, and culture and heritage protection present a more complicated environment in which to plan (and a greater propensity for land-use conflicts).

The supply of land is one of the biggest limitations when it comes to planning because of the land ownership structure of greenfield areas. During the socialist state period, Poland eliminated the right of a natural person to own property, including land. Because of this, land was not an object of transaction under the socialist state system – it was communal and state owned. However, in Poland small plots of land remained in private hands largely to support small-scale agriculture. An estimated 70% of agricultural lands were in the hands of private individuals and remained so after 1989, even in cases where they did not have the documents to prove ownership (Ney and Poczobut-Odlanicki, 1998). Consequently, rural areas tend to have long narrow plots, hundreds of subdivisions and hundreds of owners. These small plots present a major obstacle to the development of the agricultural industry which suffers from a lack of economies of scale in such cases (Sikorska, 2013).

Across Poland, approximately 50% of agricultural land is owned by farm holdings with an area smaller than 15 hectares (Kassenberg, Karaczun and Owczarek 2015: 63). That is why areas outside of communes are more efficient at providing larger parcels of land. Land consolidation and exchange are used as instruments to counteract the ongoing fragmentation of the agrarian structure of Polish – they "offer the opportunity to create diverse landscapes with conditions for multifunctional development of rural areas and thereby create additional sources of income, such as with recreation and tourism, for the population of such areas" (Kupidura et al., 2014: 313).

Nowosolna is experiencing several conflicts between existing owners and new inhabitants. There are two residential areas surrounded by agriculture which are experiencing conflict between uses, particularly with regards to animal husbandry (pigs and chicken farms). The municipality is proposing to address this by having residents who are presently in areas near pig farms sell their properties to create new investments in animal husbandry, resulting in compatible land uses. Residents would be unlikely to suffer a loss on the value of their properties and would be able to move to areas that are protected from such developments. Further, new infrastructure developments (the highway and a high-speed train) are going to transform parts of the area – residents do not have a say in these infrastructure investments which proceed according to special infrastructural acts.

The "Study on the conditions and directions of spatial development" of Nowosolna (spatial study) was prepared in 2013. As a result of the study, the 21 local spatial development plans are in the process of being changed/updated. The new plans are required because of growth in residential housing development. The north-eastern area (bordering Łódź) has the highest population density and brings the most revenue for the municipal budget. The new plans increase the population density and shift land usage from rural to residential.

The new spatial study for Nowosolna creates three general zones for development: one for a dense residential area, the northern area as a more rural landscape (agriculture and pasture) and the north-eastern part as an investment area for logistic warehouses connected to a new highway.[21] The municipality has engaged citizens in these plans from the onset at a very preliminary stage. When undertaking plans, Nowosolna has sought feedback from surrounding jurisdictions and analysed the content of planning documents elaborated by the adjacent municipalities and planning documents prepared by the Łódź *voivodship* in order to ensure complementary land-use functions.[22] Thus, both the binding law (Spatial Planning and Development Act 2003) and the good practices established within the ongoing collaboration between different communes set out the opportunities for Nowosolna to participate in the planning process activities of the adjacent municipalities. Such activities help to co-ordinate the common investments regarding technical infrastructure, transportation and public services development. Presently it was described that there are few, if any, conflicts regarding land usage with surrounding jurisdictions because of compatible zoning and practices. However, there is acknowledged competition between Nowosolna and the city of Łódź, including strong pressure for residential development.

Nowosolna plans to tackle the creation of one new plan per budgetary year. The commune will be altering the geographic scope of the new local spatial development plans and the composition of the new zones is presently in deliberation. Having a single plan for a large portion of the municipal area became problematic when one resident grieved the plan process, thus halting its development. Municipal officials have expressed that it is easier to manage with a small plan when people grieve the process. The municipality plans to adopt 13 plans in total which will entail new area divisions; the zoning structure will be changed to make it more even.

The issue of compensation for land-use zoning decisions is not expected to be a problem in this case because the new road raises the value of the land as does a plot's ability to be sold for a new purpose. Nowosolna has jurisdiction over making plans and releasing planning decisions. The only constraint to this decision-making power is the protection of environmentally sensitive areas (which is based on national law).

There are fiscal incentives for Nowosolna to increase the number of residential developments in its locale – doing so benefits the commune through per capita transfers, income and property taxes. Own-source revenues (i.e. revenues from corporate and personal income taxes and various other taxes) account of 66% of Nowosolna's total budget (Statistical Office in Łódź, 2014b). Per capita allocations from the state budget account for 9% of the total budget and state subsidies the remaining 21%. Of own-source revenues, personal income taxes are the largest contributor – accounting for 54% of all own-source revenues. Tax on real estate (or property taxes) is the second-largest contributor to own-source revenues at 25%.

While the commune is working to update and reconfigure its local land-use plans around three distinct uses, it is also developing a number of cultural assets and tourist sites related to historical monuments and places and a protected forest area. In essence, there is spatial coherence in the way the commune seeks to reorient its space – one element of which is to create a new centre for the commune within Nowosolna proper (as opposed to its historic centre in what is now Łódź).

Summary of major challenges

This case study of Łódź highlights a metropolitan area in the midst of transition. The city is being reshaped by a number of large-scale EU-funded infrastructure projects (e.g. road and rail networks) and a major urban regeneration project. It is successfully attracting new businesses/industries and private investments. The investments made today will shape the morphology of the city for years to come. Layered atop these major investments are the tandem trends of deconcentration and depopulation, which over the longer term, threaten the city's fiscal sustainability. Further, at present planning is poorly integrated across Łódź's functional area and there are few incentives to adopt multi-jurisdictional co-operation on spatial policy. The new Metropolitan Association Act creates the potential for such collaboration through municipal association.

In terms of transportation planning, Łódź is struggling with how to balance the needs of individual users and promote the public and sustainable transportation options (especially in the city centre). The city will need to integrate the new road and rail infrastructure into existing networks as it seeks to create a coherent, intermodal and regional transport network which emphasises public transportation (especially rail transport).

The major issues facing residential planning are (as described in the spatial study) to increase the attractiveness and quality of life in the centre of the city. Most importantly, the revitalisation of tenement houses in the historic urban core which will require a co-ordinated response across self-government departments due to a concentration of lower income residents in the area. This process needs to be managed very carefully such that vulnerable residents are not further marginalised in the process. Residential planning further needs to direct new developments more efficiently and manage the provision of land for development in the context of diminished demand for housing due to depopulation processes.

Other major planning challenges for the city include how to deal with constraints in the supply of affordable industrial lands for large developers, competition pressure from the adjoining/nearby municipalities and how to position the city in terms of co-operation/competition within the metropolitan region. Municipal officials further articulated a need for a viable policy to redevelop brownfield sites in the inner city area. For agricultural lands, production is presently inefficient within the city borders (due to a combination of historic parcellation and low soil quality). This, combined with growing urbanisation pressure due to demand for single-family housing and a low level of planning control, is causing the loss of open space, fragmentation of natural habitats, fragmentation of the city airing corridors and a loss of rural landscape (Poławski, 2009). The city seeks viable mechanisms to protect its agricultural areas via other uses.

Responses to these challenges are described in the city's spatial study which advocates for a compact urban form, the protection of greenspaces, parks, cultural and heritage sites, and the development of brownfield sites in advance of greenfield ones. But at present the city has limited tools to realise these stated aims and there are contradictions embedded in the planning system which detract from its effectiveness.

Notes

1. The term "urban sprawl" is used to denote the process of urban expansion to the city outskirts by more than what might be socially desirable. Most experts seem to agree that fragmentation of urbanised areas, increased mobility needs and low population density are the most significant features of urban sprawl. Urban sprawl can pose

significant threats to the environment. Higher emissions of CO_2 and air pollutants, lower water quality, loss of biodiversity, and a reduction of open space comprise only a few examples of the possible effects of urban sprawl. On the other hand, urban sprawl may also entail reduced risks to human health and social welfare, mainly stemming from lower population density. Examples of such risks include population exposure to air pollutants, natural hazards (e.g. floods, storms, etc.) and epidemics. See OECD (2014).

2. The Łódź region (*voivodeship*) is the ninth-largest in the country in term of size (18 200 km²), and has a total population of roughly 2.5 million inhabitants (2014). The region consists of 24 districts (including 3 urban districts which account for 34.1% of the population and 21 rural districts) and 177 communes (18 urban, 26 urban-rural and 133 rural). Łódź is the seat of both the regional and local government.

3. As a recent OECD working paper notes: "The high mortality rate results are mostly among people between the ages of 20-50 and due to cardiovascular diseases, rates which are 40-80% higher than they are in the rest of Poland. However, this high mortality rate can also be connected to results regarding the assessment of quality of life, which indicate that the inhabitants of the Łódzkie region, together with the inhabitants of the Lublin region, are least satisfied with their living conditions and show the lowest levels of optimism when considering their future prospects. Cardiovascular mortality is primarily the result of man-made diseases, so it is recommended that public authorities increase inhabitants' awareness of cardiovascular diseases and promote healthier lifestyles" (Szukalski, Martinez-Fernandez and Weyman, 2013: 16).

4. In Łódź, this amounts to 25%, as opposed to 42% in Brzeziny district, 28% in Zgierz district, 27% in Pabianice district and 25% in Eastern Łódź (Statistical Office in Łódź, 2014b).

5. These are concentrated in several areas, four of which are detached from the urban centre (Widzew, Retkinia, Teofilów and Radogoszcz) and form a self-sufficient territory with their own public services. Others are integrated with the city, e.g. Bałuty, Dąbrowa, Chojny, Zarzew and Wielkopolska. The fate of these buildings is linked to the socio-economic status of their owners; buildings with a large number of senior residents who rely on state pensions tend to have a greater tendency to be run down than those with a larger working age population who can better afford their upkeep. Despite this characterisation, housing remains desirable (Marcińczak and Sagan, 2011).

6. This information is based on the European Union's Corine land cover inventory. Land cover statistics for functional urban areas were compiled using raster images from the Corine project and vector files that indicate boundaries of territorial units. Given the specifications of the land cover files, the number of pixels of a certain colour within a territory corresponds to the area in hectares covered by a land cover class. Pixel counts for each territory were imported into statistical software for analysis.

7. This includes the north-eastern fringes of the city surrounding the Łódź Hights Landscape Park and Nowosolna area; the southern areas in the vicinity of Ruda Pabianicka; and Stare Zlotno at the western fringes of the city.

8. In the Olechow-Janow area.

9. Uchwała Nr 218/2008. Prezydium Państwowej Komisji Akredytacyjnej z dnia 10 kwietnia 2008 r, http://a.umed.pl/procesbolonski/materialy/PKA_kryteria_studenckie.pdf.

10. It should be noted that the Łódź Voivodeship also has a development strategy – the regional strategy notes that its implementation falls on the local governments (Development Strategy for the Region of Łódź 2007-2020). This strategy was updated for the new EU programming period 2014-20 and adopted once again by Łódź Voivodeship Sejmik in 2013. Its name changed to the Development Strategy for the Łódźkie Region 2020).

11. Łódź also has a "Strategy of promotion and marketing communication of the Łódź brand for the years 2010-2016" which describes the strategic goals of development of Łódź as a creative city (the strategy was ratified by the City Council in 2011). The city has undertaken a number of creative projects such as: "Mia100 Kamienic" (A City of 100 Tenement Houses), "Łódź Rewitalizuje" (Łódź Revitalizes Itself), "Mam pomysł na biznes" (I Have a Business Idea), "Art Inkubator w Fabryce Sztuki" (Art Incubator in a Factory of Art) and "Lokale Dla Kreatywnych" (Premises for the Creatives).

12. The other pillars are: 1) economy and infrastructure; 2) society and culture.

13. Act on Special Economic Zones of 20 October 1994 (Journal of Laws of 2007, No. 42, item 274, Journal of Laws of 2008, No. 118, item 746).

14. The special economic zones in Poland and are run by the Ministry of Economic Development together with regional governments. The city of Łódź is a part shareholder in the special economic zone for its region.

15. Property taxation based on size (as opposed to value) was first legislated on the 1991 bill on local taxation. This system has remained largely unchanged since then. The property tax on land is calculated per square metre and on buildings per square metre of usable surface.

16. For example the Łódź Agency of Regional Development, which provides services to both public and private regional actors. The agency provides advisory services to local authorities to help them access EU structural funds, as well as assistance with the implementation of ERDF-funded projects; assistance with design and planning, implementation and monitoring of development strategies, local development programmes, as well as local feasibility studies of projects, which apply for EU funding.

17. At present, detailed data for Łódź are published every two years; there is an overall publication on the statistics of Łódź and short-term data are also released on a quarterly basis. GDP data for the region are published every two years with a gap between the year of referencing and that of publishing, which limits the timeliness of the data. Data concerning land use are published annually – data on building permits and on some residential buildings are published on a monthly basis. Indicators on industry migration, demography and the labour market are provided quarterly. Data on housing prices are available at a regional level and are published by regional offices. Income data are available from the household survey.

18. The urban regeneration process was the main focus of a recent conference of the association of urban planning professionals, which promotes best practices related to sustainable planning and public engagement.

19. The city of Łódź does not have districts – they were abolished in 2010 when the city was restructured. The main rationale for this was to reduce administration. Under the old system, the old historical city of Łódź was split between two districts, which made it difficult to gather data and analyse trends and districts tended to have different spatial policies and compete with each other, rather than be part of one unified plan.

20. The OECD has forwarded a programme of research based on this perspective, seeing urban and rural not as a dichotomy, but as interconnected spaces that are best thought of in unison if one is to achieve the goals of sustainable development. This is based on analysis of the functional linkages of these spaces through, for instance, commuting flows. In a similar vein, the European Union advocates for planning to encompass both urban and rural areas in unison so as to achieve more effective land-use planning, including better provision of services and more effective management of natural resources. This has also been prevalent in the work of the United Nations and in particular the UN Human Settlements Program (UN-Habitat).

21. Developments on agricultural lands that exceed one hectare on a particular arable grade of land (as stated in the Act on Protection of Agricultural and Forest Land, 1995) require permission from the relevant agricultural authority.

22. As outlined in the Spatial Planning and Development Act 2003, neighbouring municipalities can submit proposals for planning documents; issue opinions and submit comments to the drafts of planning documents; participate in public purpose investment consultations. Municipalities may also consider the development trends of neighbouring municipalities within their own planning processes.

Bibliography

Alterman (2010), *Takings international: A comparative perspective on land use regulations and compensation rights*, American Bar Association.

Brzeziński, C. (2010), Procesy suburbanizacji obszarów podmiejskich na przykładzie gmin powiatu pabianickiego, *Zmiany przestrzenne.*

Central Statistical Office of Poland (2014), "Population projection 2014-2050", http://stat.gov.pl/en/topics/population/population-projection/population-projection-2014-2050,2,5.html (accessed 25 April 2016).

City of Lódz (2015), Ustalanie w drodze decyzji lokalizacji inwestycji celu publicznego i warunków zabudowy, http://bip.uml.Lódz.pl/index.php?str=23&id=775 (accessed 25 March 2016).

City of Łódź (2012), Integrated Development Strategy for Lodz 2020+, Resolution No. XLIII/824/12 of the City Council in Łódź of 25 June 2012, http://bip.uml.lodz.pl/_plik.php?id=35030 (accessed 25 March 2016).

City of Lódz (2011), Integrated Development Strategy of Łódź 2020+/Strategia Zintegrowanego Rozwoju Łodzi 2020+, http://uml.lodz.pl/miasto/strategia (accessed 25 March 2016).

City of Łódź (2010), Studium uwarunkowań i kierunków zagospodarowania przestrzennego miasta Łódźi.

Dale-Johnson, D., and W.J. Brzeski (2001), "Land value functions and land price indexes in Cracow, 1993–1999", *Journal of Housing Economics*, Vol. 10(3), pp. 307-334.

Expander (2016), "Raport Metrohouse i Expandera – Kwiecień 2016", Expander, www.expander.pl/aktualnosci/rynek_nieruchomosci/17055,wiadomosc.html#news_17055 (accessed 25 March 2016).

Habitat for Humanity (2015), "Housing review 2015: Affordability, livability, sustainability", Habitat for Humanity, Bratislava, www.habitat.org/sites/default/files/housing_review_2015_full_report_final_small_reduced.pdf.

Havel, M.B. (2014), "Delineation of property rights as institutional foundations for urban land markets in transition", *Land Use Policy*, Vol. 38, pp. 615-626, http://dx.doi.org/10.1016/j.landusepol.2014.01.004.

Healey, P. (2006), "Territory, integration and spatial planning", in: Tewdwr-Jones, M. and P. Allmendinger (eds.), *Territory, Identity and Spatial Planning: Spatial Governance in a Fragmented Nation*, Routledge, pp. 64-79.

Invest in Poland (2015), "Łódź special economic zone", Polish Information and Foreign Investment Agency, Warsaw, www.paiz.gov.pl/investment_support/sez/lodz (accessed 25 March 2016).

Izdebski, H., A. Nelicki and I. Zachariasz (2007), "Polish regulatory framework and democratic rule of law", Ernst & Young.

Kassenberg, A., Z. Karaczun and D. Owczarek (2015), *Sustainable Development Goals and Indicators for a Small Planet: Securing Means of Implementation in Poland, An Output of the Asia-Europe Environment Forum (ENVforum)*, Asia-Europe Foundation, Singapore, www.asef.org/images/docs/Polish%20Case%20Study.pdf.

Kupidura, A. et al. (2014), "Public perceptions of rural landscapes in land consolidation procedures in Poland", *Land Use Policy*, Vol. 39, pp. 313-319, http://dx.doi.org/10.1016/j.landusepol.2014.02.005.

Lamprecht, M. (2014), "Urban land use planning", in: Marszal, T. (ed.), *Spatial Development of Contemporary Poland in Łódź*, Łódź University Press, Łódź, Poland, pp. 61-89, available at: http://dspace.uni.lodz.pl:8080/xmlui/bitstream/handle/11089/5530/Lamprecht_URBAN%20LAND%20USE%20PLANNING.pdf?sequence=1.

Lasinska, K. (2013), *Social Capital in Eastern Europe: Poland an Exception?*, Springer Science and Business Media.

Łódź Regional Government (2006), The Development Strategy for the Lódź Region, for the Years 2007-2020.

Marcińczak, S. and I. Sagan (2011), "The socio-spatial restructuring of Łódź, Poland", *Urban Studies*, Vol. 48/9, pp. 1 789-1 809, http://dx.doi.org/10.1177/0042098010379276.

Ministry for Infrastructure and Development (n.d.), "Integrated territorial investments: New solutions for cities in the Cohesion Policy 2014-2020", Ministry for

Infrastructure and Development, Warsaw, www.mir.gov.pl/media/9914/Broszura_ENG.pdf.

Narodowy Bank Polski (2016), "Information on home prices and the situation in housing and commercial real estate market in Poland in 2015 Q4", Financial Stability Department, Narodowy Bank Polski, March, www.nbp.pl/en/publikacje/inne/real_estate_market_2015_Q4.pdf.

New Centre of Lódz (2015), "100 hectares in the heart of the city", presentation.

Ney, B. and A. Poczobut-Odlanicki (1998), "Property rights and rights to the value of land in Poland: Current situation following changes in the years 1944-1998", in: Domański, R. (ed.), *Emerging Spatial and Regional Structures of an Economy in Transition*: *Studia Regionalia*, Vol. 8, Polish Academy of Science, Committee for Space Economy and Regional Planning, Warsaw.

OECD (2016), "Regional well-being indictors, Lódzkie region", www.oecdregionalwellbeing.org/PL11.html.

OECD (2015), *OECD Metropolitan Areas Database*, Metropolitan eXplorer, http://measuringurban.oecd.org.

OECD (2014), "Effectiveness of spatial and land use policies in achieving environmental and economic objectives", ENV/EPOC/WPIEEP(2014)18, OECD, Paris.

OECD (2013), *Rural-Urban Partnerships: An Integrated Approach to Economic Development*, OECD Publishing, Paris, http://dx.doi.org/10.1787/9789264204812-en.

OECD (2011a), "OECD extended regional typology", OECD, Paris, www.oecd.org/gov/regional-policy/48670214.pdf.

OECD (2011b), *OECD Urban Policy Reviews, Poland 2011*, OECD Publishing, Paris, http://dx.doi.org/10.1787/9789264097834-en.

OECD (2010), *OECD Economic Surveys: Poland 2010*, OECD Publishing, Paris, http://dx.doi.org/10.1787/eco_surveys-pol-2010-en.

Poławski, Z.F. (2009), "Zmiany użytkowania ziemi w Polsce w ostatnich dwóch stuleciach", *Teledetekcja środowiska*, Vol. 42, pp. 69-82, http://geoinformatics.uw.edu.pl/wp-content/uploads/sites/26/2014/03/TS_v42_Polawski.pdf.

Polish Information and Foreign Investment Agency (2015), "Construction process", webpage, www.paiz.gov.pl/polish_law/construction_process (accessed 25 March 2016).

Regulamin Organizacyjny urzedu Miasta Lodzi, Zalacznik do zarzadzenia Nr 1964/VI/12, Prezydenta Miasta Lodzi z dnia 21 marca 2012 r, http://bip.uml.lodz.pl/_plik.php?id=30546.

Sagan, I. and M. Grabkowska (2012), "Urban regeneration in Gdańsk, Poland: Local regimes and tensions between top-down strategies and endogenous renewal", *European Planning Studies*, Vol. 20/7, pp. 1 135-1 154, http://dx.doi.org/10.1080/09654313.2012.674347.

Sikorska, A. (2013), Przemiany w strukturze agrarnej indywidualnych gospodarstw rolnych, *Instytut Ekonomiki Rolnictwa i Gospodarki Żywnościowej-Państwowy Instytut Badawczy.*

Śleszyński, P. (2014), "Distribution of population density in Polish towns and cities", *Geogrphica Polonica*, Vol. 87/1, pp. 61-75, http://dx.doi.org/10.7163/GPol.2014.4.

Statistical Office in Łódź (2014a), *Statistics of Łódź 2014*, Statistical Office in Łódź, http://lodz.stat.gov.pl/en/publications/statistical-yearbook/statistics-of-lodz-2014,1,11.html (accessed 25 March 2016).

Statistical Office in Łódź (2014b), *Lódzkie Voivodship 2014: Subregions, Powiats, Gminas*, Statistical Office in Łódź, http://lodz.stat.gov.pl/en/publications/statistical-yearbook/lodzkie-voivodship-2014-subregions-powiats-gminas,2,16.html.

Szukalski, P., C. Martinez-Fernandez and T. Weyman (2013), "Lódzkie region: Demographic challenges within an ideal location", *OECD Local Economic and Employment Development (LEED) Working Papers*, No. 2013/05, OECD Publishing, Paris, http://dx.doi.org/10.1787/5k4818gt720p-en.

Vigar, G. (2009), "Towards an integrated spatial planning",? *European Planning Studies*, Vol. 17/11, pp. 1 571-1 590, http://dx.doi.org/10.1080/09654310903226499.

Warzywoda-Kruszyńska, W. and A. Golczyńska-Grondas (2010), Wzmocnić szanse i osłabić transmisję biedy wśród mieszkańców miast województwa łódzkiego-Wzlot:(raport końcowy+ rekomendacje), Instytut Socjologii Uniwersytetu Łódzkiego.

Warzywoda-Kruszyńska, W., Jankowski, B., Grotowska-Leder, J. and E. Rokicka, (2013), Łódzka Szkoła Badań Ubóstwa.

World Bank (2015), *Doing Business in Poland 2015*, World Bank Group, Washington, DC, www.doingbusiness.org/~/media/GIAWB/Doing%20Business/Documents/Subnational-Reports/DB15-Poland.pdf.

Chapter 3.

Towards more effective and inclusive land-use governance in Łódź

This final chapter offers an assessment of how land is governed in Łódź and recommendations on how to improve upon the present system. It assesses the multi-level system of spatial planning and capacity at the local level. It analyses the various instruments for land-use planning and how they work together, and notes the instruments that are not presently being used, but potentially could be. Following this, some of the major issues facing the area are discussed, including how to more effectively co-ordinate with surrounding rural municipalities, engage citizens in participatory planning, and address the tandem challenges of depopulation and sprawl.

The statistical data for Israel are supplied by and under the responsibility of the relevant Israeli authorities. The use of such data by the OECD is without prejudice to the status of the Golan Heights, East Jerusalem and Israeli settlements in the West Bank under the terms of international law.

The preceding chapters have described the legislative, regulatory and fiscal environment that shapes spatial planning and development in Poland and have illustrated planning in practice through the case of Łódź and its surrounding locales. Over the past two and a half decades Poland's system of spatial planning has evolved considerably. The country has introduced new legal frameworks to establish property rights and manage real-estate transactions and has outlined the competencies of the different levels of government to spatially plan. This has accompanied decentralisation – local government empowerment and the creation of a regional governmental tier.

Each reform has built on what were seen as previous inadequacies in the system. The most recent legislation guiding spatial planning in the country – the Spatial Planning and Development Act 2003 and its subsequent amendments (e.g. June 2010) – simplified some planning procedures. The recent Acts on Metropolitan Association and Urban Revitalisation (2015) support the need for planning across functional urban areas and enable more tools to implement urban revitalisation projects along with strong accountability mechanisms and public engagement in decision making. In line with the Leipzig Charter, the national level is setting direction for urban development and creating new mechanisms to support the goals of sustainable development and well-being. The recently adopted National Urban Policy in 2023 identifies many deficiencies in the current system and sets a strong direction for future reforms.[1] These are all positive developments.

However, many challenges remain. Much of the scholarship on these issues has focused on the substance of plans and strategies and their accompanying policy tools. As one researcher notes, "Polish municipalities in general do not pursue an *active* land policy in the sense that in the sense of acquiring the land, planning and putting in an infrastructure and then disposing ready plots to building developers" (Havel, 2014: 622). Instead, developments tend to proceed on a case-by-case basis, with public authorities responsible for utilities and little else (Havel, 2014: 622). This type of land development by single case has been particularly criticised for its inability to manage sprawl. For example, a 2013 study by Kowalewski et al. on the economic and social costs of uncontrolled urbanisation in Poland finds that the current regulatory, plan-based system is increasingly incapable of managing the urbanisation processes – in the words of the authors, the present system "results in "spatial chaos and a waste of space and capital". The lack of fiscal tools to manage land uses are also of great importance. Given these challenges and inadequacies, there is an appetite for further change in the planning system. This is substantiated by the literature on spatial and land-use planning in Poland, including the OECD's *Environmental Performance Review* (2015a) and *Territorial Review* (2008b).[2] The present system is ripe for improvement – a fact that the government has long acknowledged and continues to work towards (Government of Poland, 2007).

This chapter describes the major issues and presents an analysis of the planning system based on the case study of Łódź. It analyses how land use is governed, including the formal "nested" system of spatial planning, how the different scales work together, their major aims and objectives, and the ways in which fiscal and regulatory tools are presently used to shape land use.

Multi-level spatial planning

The strategies at the national, regional and local levels are meant to guide and inform one another. These strategies describe the major trends and challenges facing spatial planning and analyse a wide range of indicators in order to inform practice. However, the present regulatory and planning framework has embedded within it a number of inadequacies and inconsistencies which challenge the realisation of core objectives.

At the national level, the National Spatial Development Concept 2030 (NSDC) has six major objectives: to improve the competitiveness of major urban centres within the European space while at the same time retaining polycentric settlement structures; to promote functional spatial integration; to improve transport and telecommunications infrastructure; to maintain the natural environment and landscape; to promote energy security and environmental hazard protection; and finally, to restore and consolidate the spatial planning system (Government of Poland, 2012). The NSDC includes high-level maps to illustrate various aspects of spatial development (e.g. energy systems, commuting flows, local spatial development plan coverage). These types of illustrative maps are common for national spatial plans in OECD countries. One interesting exception to this is Israel, which has adopted a language of "textures" to forward planning objectives and whose national spatial plans contain far more detailed maps than is typical (Box 3.1).

Box 3.1. **National spatial planning: The use of "textures" in Israel**

Israel's spatial planning is unique among OECD countries – the national government plays a very strong role by forwarding detailed regional plans. Israel's National Master Plan No. 35, approved in 2005, is a general spatial plan which adopts the methodology of sustainable development by balancing between development and preservation. It is primarily a map-based zoning plan at a scale of 1:100 000 and contains general guidelines and strategic elements only as secondary aspects. The statutory component of the plan highlights such principles as contiguous development, minimum density for residential uses, urban regeneration and open space protection. While it has the same legal status as all other national outline plans, in practice it is considered to have an overriding status. It also provides the zoning regulations that lower level plans have to follow, except in areas that are covered by flexibility clauses. The plan includes a clause that prohibits all developments outside of existing urban boundaries, but recent reforms have introduced exemptions that can be granted by a special national body.

The plan develops a new common and more flexible planning language – the language of "textures" – that identifies and distinguishes between development-oriented and preservation-oriented areas. These textures are demarcated planning areas, like zones, in which a variety of land uses are permissible and others are restricted. The map and instructions of NMP 35 divide the country into five texture typologies: urban texture, rural texture, mixed preserved texture, national preserved texture and coastal texture. Each texture includes instructions which regulate built areas for residence and employment, open space and infrastructure systems. The textures differ from one another in the quantitative and spatial relations between land uses and their designations, in their development and preservation levels, and in the rules governing and directing these relations. At the same time, it promotes public transportation, facilitates the reduction of social gaps, calls for the integration of infrastructure corridors and emphasises environmental sustainability. Overall, the language of textures enables a clear definition of restrictions while providing flexibility, without the need to draw development borders for isolated localities or to establish population targets for each locality on an individual basis.

As in many OECD countries, Israel is currently in the process of attempting to simplify its planning system. The development of the National Master Plan No. 1 is currently under process. This reform aims to unify all 47 national master plans, as well as the hundreds of partial plans incorporating changes within them, in order to provide policy makers with readable, simple and coherent national statutory information relevant to each and every piece of land and major planning challenge.

Sources: Government of Israel (2015), "Integrated planning in Israel", www.moin.gov.il/Subjects/GeneralPlaning/Pages/default.aspx; Assif, S. (2007), "Principles of Israel's Comprehensive National Outline Plan for Construction, Development and Conservation (NOP 35)", www.moin.gov.il/SubjectDocuments/Tma35_PrinciplesDocument.pdf.

Regional spatial development plans forward complementary objectives to that of national ones – for the Łódź region this includes socio-economic development, regional competitiveness and functional spatial planning. At the local level, the spatial study based on an analysis of relevant local indicators and trends guides practice – a process that one academic study describes as time-consuming, expensive, and "part of a long lasting political game" (Holuj and Zawilińska, 2013: 125). Łódź's spatial strategy aims to create a compact urban form, retain the city's historical character, and protect its greenspace and natural environments.

The links between the spatial policies at the regional and local levels are tenuous. The spatial studies are meant to inform one another, but there are limited monitoring/enforcement mechanisms to ensure that they do so (see Box 3.2 for an illustration of this issue in the Podlaskie region). In particular, the regional spatial development plans are meant to act as an instrument to inform evidence-based planning practice, including functional connections/interactions between locales in order to facilitate inter municipal co-ordination. However, these plans are not binding on municipalities and thus tend to remain general in application. While municipalities are required to undertake studies on the conditions and directions for local land-use management and most municipalities have undertaken this work, the resulting studies do not have binding force. Further, there are situations where proposed spatial policies are not supported in any way by prevailing economic conditions (Holuj and Zawilińska, 2013: 123). This issue is elaborated upon in the following section.

The National Spatial Development Concept 2030 and regional plans encourage a functional understanding of metropolitan areas – but local planning does not adopt this view. Local governments have limited opportunity or incentives to adopt such a perspective. The new Metropolitan Association Act creates a legal basis for the harmonisation of different plans with spatial implications across the functional urban area. This is a positive development.

The spatial planning documents at the national and regional scales contain a wide range of recommendations and objectives which are the purview of the local level. Many of these recommendations include suggestions for reforms which local governments at present have no ability to direct. The NSDC in particular highlights a number of inadequacies in the present system for which local governments experience constraints. It thus serves as a strategy which describes planning objectives, but also points out the inadequacies of the current system and suggests directions for reform.

Local planning objectives and capacity

Planners in Łódź seek a compact urban form which protects cultural and heritage assets, preserves its historical industrial architecture, and protects the city's greenspace such that brownfield sites are developed in advance of greenfield ones. The case study has revealed many promising practices, including urban regeneration, heritage and parks protection, the creation of attractive city spaces, and a growing culture of public participation in the planning process. However, the case study of Łódź also reveals the numerous constraints facing the planning system. Planners in Łódź, as in the rest of Poland, have relatively limited tools at their disposal to shape development: they are largely limited to regulatory local spatial development plans or the creation of non-binding strategic documents (i.e. spatial study). To this end, the planning framework could be strengthened by enhancing the role of the spatial study; increasing plan coverage and eliminating the planning decision mechanism; remedying legal ambiguities; and expanding the suite of planning of tools available.

Box 3.2. Lessons from land-use planning in Podlaskie Voivodeship

A 2013 audit of environmental land practices in Podlaskie Voivodeship by the Supreme Audit Office provides an illustrative example of some of the conditions that are affecting land-use planning across Poland.

The audit found that local governments in the *voivodeship* are not protecting natural areas and that local governments do not, in practice, conduct land-use policy. The audit found that only 15% of the province is covered by a local spatial development plan, the majority of which were outdated. Land-use planning studies – which are required by law under the Land User Planning Act – were also found to be outdated. In the absence of up-to-date plans, land-use decisions are dominated by the planning decision process and as a result, investors' decisions are shaping land use, rather than public policy.

The audit further found that regulatory mechanisms for monitoring and evaluation are not often used in practice. The vast majority of plans related to nature reserves and protected landscapes were outdated, e.g. they did not bear mention of Natura 2000 reserves.[1] It was further reported that the audited municipalities do not analyse (and report on) changes to land development in their areas, nor do they evaluate their progress in developing local plans.

It was found that 40% of the municipalities in the *voivodeship* do not charge land-use planning fees even though these levies are required by law. This fee is used to capture the change in the value of land when a property is sold. The audit also found that county construction inspectors do not properly respond to cases of violation.

As a result of this analysis, the National Audit Office recommends that local governments in Podlaskie Voivodeship: 1) draft and implement plans as soon as possible; 2) that local land-use studies and plans be made compliant with the Spatial Planning and Development Act 2003 and the Environmental Protection Act; 3) that fees related to the change in the value of the land be collected.

Note: 1. Natura 2000 is the centrepiece of the European Union's nature and biodiversity network. It was established under the 1992 Habitats Directive which aims to assure the long-term survival of Europe's most valuable and threatened species and habitats.

Source: Najwyższa Izba Kontroli (2013), Lokalizacja inwestycji na obszarach objętych ochroną przyrody w województwie Podlaskim, Informacja o wynikach kontroli, www.nik.gov.pl/plik/id,7229,vp,9113.pdf.

Łódź's spatial study – which is equivalent to comprehensive or strategic plans in other countries – puts forward a model of urbanisation. Such strategic plans are meant to capture social, economic and environmental characteristics, and reflect their spatial consequences both now and into the future. They are at once a "snapshot" of multiple spatial interactions; a projection of how they will evolve over time (sometimes this can include multiple scenarios); a set of indicators to monitor progress; and a normative vision of how development should proceed (a social contract of sorts). They can be very powerful tools both to understand urban systems now and in the future and orient development towards strategic goals. In Łódź, and in Polish cities more generally, the role of this spatial study as a strategic document is an important guide for future development, but it could be used to do more; the spatial study contains strong analysis, but its implementation, monitoring and evaluation mechanisms should be strengthened. In the longer term, the document's status as a non-binding study should be reconsidered. As the main overarching document for the city's spatial development, it could achieve more if it had greater regulatory heft.

The need for better monitoring mechanisms has been raised by other analyses of the planning system in Łódź.[3] There are a number of ways this function could be strengthened. For instance, given that densification is a clearly stated objective for Łódź's future development, monitoring indicators tied to targets should be a part of the city's spatial study. The OECD's comparative work in this area (OECD, 2012) has demonstrated a range of approaches to achieving these objectives and has proposed indicators that can be used to mark their progress (Table 3.1).

Table 3.1. **Core compact city indicators**

Category		Indicator	Description
Indicators related to compactness	Dense and proximate development patterns	Population and urban land growth	Annual growth rate of population and urban land within a metropolitan area
		Population density and urban land	Population over the surface of urban land within a metropolitan area
		Retrofitting existing urban land	Share of development that occurs on existing urban land rather than on greenfield land
		Intensive use of buildings	Vacancy rates of housing and offices
		Housing form	Share of multi-family houses in total housing units
		Trip distance	Average trip distance for commuting/all trips
		Urban land cover	Share of urban land in a metropolitan area
	Urban areas linked by public transport systems	Trips using public transport	Share of trips using public transport (for commuting/for all trips) in total trips
		Proximity to public transport	Share of population (and/or employment) within walking distance (e.g. 500 meters) of public transport stations in total population
	Accessibility to local services and jobs	Matching jobs and homes	Balance between jobs and homes at the neighbourhood scale
		Matching public services and homes	Balance between local services and homes at the neighbourhood scale
		Proximity to local services	Share of population within walking distance (e.g. 500 meters) of local services
		Trips on foot and by bicycle	Share of trips on foot and by bicycle (for commuting/for all trips) in total trips
Indicators related to the impact of compact city policies	Environmental	Public space and green areas	Share of population within walking distance (e.g. 500 meters) of green space accessible to the public
		Transport energy use	Transport energy consumption per capita
		Residential energy use	Residential energy consumption per capita
	Social	Affordability	Share of household expenditure on housing and transport in total housing expenditure
	Economic	Public services	Expenditure on maintaining urban infrastructure (roads, water facilities, etc.) per capita

Source: OECD (2012), *Compact City Policies: A Comparative Assessment*, http://dx.doi.org/10.1787/9789264167865-en.

Łódź's integrated development strategy (City of Łódź, 2012) also has a role to play in this regard. It is a communications tool between city officials and citizens to raise awareness about directions for development. It is described as a first step towards implementing a strategic and operational management system for the various organisational units in the city and accompanying this, a programme of implementation along with programme monitoring and evaluation. These functions should certainly be developed as soon as possible given the rapid pace of the city's development. It is also important that other sectoral plans which affect land use are considered in tandem: for example, transportation plans, economic development plans and strategies for climate adaptation, mitigation and disaster preparedness.

One of the most important issues facing Łódź – and many other cities across Poland – is its low local spatial development plan coverage. This lack of coverage facilitates urban sprawl and is contrary to the spatial development objectives of the city.[4] Local spatial development plans are important tools to manage conflict between competing uses and in order to set out clear parameters for future development. They provide the foundations for an agreement between citizens and their government on how land-use decisions in their locale will proceed. In the absence of this, residents, developers and businesses do not have a clear signal on if, when and where developments will occur. Moreover, fragmented developments can make it hard for local governments to deliver good infrastructure and services in a cost-effective manner. Both city representatives and representatives from the development industry were in favour of extending the coverage of local plans. However, the process is described as long, complex and risky due to the prospect for citizens to claim compensation from the municipality for any reduced value in other property as a result of a local plan. The litigious and procedurally imbalanced nature of this process hampers plan adoption. Ideally, all municipalities in Poland should be covered by detailed, up-to-date local spatial development plans that have been approved through meaningful public involvement. This would give investors a reliable and stable understanding of the requirements and would give the municipality a consistent basis on which to reject or approve changes in land use or construction permits according to overarching spatial development goals.

Where municipalities have adopted local spatial development plans, this accompanies a legal requirement to provide the necessary infrastructure to support developments. However, given the structure of local finances, such investments in most cases would result in a very marginal increase in direct tax revenue; gains in personal or income tax would take time to be realised and would be unlikely to cover infrastructure costs (Radzimski, 2012: 671). Given this, there are disincentives for municipalities to adopt plans (because of obligations associated with them) or undertake new infrastructure investments unless there are special funds allocated to these activities. Municipalities thus seek to avoid long-term financial obligations and adopt "incremental planning" instead – resulting in infrastructure shortages in suburban areas, automobile dependency and congestion (Radzimski, 2012: 671). Beyond these issues it is important to note that increasing the coverage of local spatial development plans may not, in and of itself, set Łódź on the path of meeting its goals for a denser urban form. A 2013 study on land-use planning by Kowalewski et al. (2013) finds that local spatial development plans alone allow an estimated 62 million residential settlements across Poland – far exceeding any potential demand. Therefore, the content of the plans matters greatly.

Beyond the role of plans, there are a number of ambiguities in the application of planning law which presently hamper the system. The Polish system places an emphasis on property rights – it did so from the onset prior to the establishment of a functioning urban land market (Havel, 2014). However, a strong system of property rights and development rights exists without an accompanying planning framework to direct such investments: developments are in essence market-led. In many places, such as Łódź, this has led to fragmented and unplanned developments that are difficult for the local government to service along with the attendant fiscal implications. There is presently confusion between development rights and property rights; these rights are not clearly defined in the Constitution and the Spatial Planning and Development Act 2003 and as a result, it often falls to the courts to adjudicate. The potential of property owners to seek compensation for any planning decision made creates a 'litigation chill' over the adoption of new plans. Better rules need to be developed regarding the issue of compensation, including how broad the compensation rights should be. The Polish Constitution does not contain provisions, such as in Article 14 of the German Constitution, that the property of land is also a source of obligation. A separate issue is the legal proviso that a development can proceed if it is in the character of the surrounding neighbourhood. The ill-defined nature of proximity within this proviso permits new developments that may not be desired. Such ambiguities detract from the effectiveness of land-use planning and send unclear signals to citizens and developers.

Presently, regulatory instruments such as development moratoria, greenbelts/urban growth boundaries, urban service boundaries, rate of growth controls are not used (see Table 3.2 for a description). Cities are not empowered to draw on such instruments under the current system. Furthermore, such instruments would be effective only if they were embedded within a metropolitan framework, as otherwise they would encourage "leapfrog" development beyond Łódź's municipal boundaries. The new Metropolitan Association Act (2015) offers some possibilities in this regard. In Łódź, the city's sprawling form and development encroachment on greenfield sites are evidence that its planning objectives are not being met. A comprehensive approach to land-use planning is still needed and a broader raft of regulatory instruments along with planning across the functional urban area can help in this regard.

Table 3.2. **Regulatory instruments: Examples**

Name of instrument	Description
Development moratorium	A development moratorium is a temporary prohibition of a particular development activity, such as building permits. This is usually done to limit development until a time when adequate public facilities may be developed. Procedurally this may require amendments to a zoning ordinance.
Greenbelt/urban growth boundary	Greenbelts refer to a land-use designation which prevents developments surrounding an urban area in order to encourage natural areas and/or agricultural land. The term "greenwedges" or "greenways" are also used to refer to the same practice for areas that do not necessarily surround a whole area, but only part of it. In essence, these tools establish a distinct boundary with separate uses around a given geography. Greenbelts are also sometimes referred to as urban growth areas/boundaries. In the United States, Oregon is the most well-known state for employing such a system state wide since 1973. All cities in Oregon are required to delineate urban land and these are kept separate from agricultural land. This is done based on a 20-year planning period.
Rate of growth controls	Rate of growth controls place an upper limit on the number of building permits issued annually, thus limiting developments.
Urban service boundary	Urban service boundaries (or areas) are an urban containment policy where certain urban services will not be provided to areas beyond the boundary. The high costs of private infrastructure for sewer and water can thus create a disincentive for developments beyond the boundary.

Finally, interviewees in Łódź noted that some of the most effective and novel projects that have been undertaken over the past few years have been based on pilot project initiatives that have engaged citizens, non-governmental organisations and other groups. Thus, more flexible arrangements have built planning capacity, both within the government and through relationships with external actors. Governments should think about how they might enhance provisions for pilot project initiatives to better integrate land-use management and economic planning. These are promising practices that should be encouraged.

Box 3.3. Counteracting urban sprawl: France's "15 km rule"

In 2000, France created a "15 km" rule to counteract urban sprawl. It mandated that any municipality located within 15 km from the outer limit of an urban agglomeration would lose its right to elaborate a land-use plan and give building permits if it is not covered by a territorial coherence plan (*Schéma de Cohérence Territoriale,* SCoT) – a form of inter-municipal plan whereby municipalities commit themselves to integrated and joint development. This rule created a very strong incentive for municipalities to join the SCoT, but it was not enough to limit urban sprawl from persisting. Writing in 2014, a government note on the matter comments that only 20% of the territory was at that time covered by an enforceable SCoT, and that their coverage was not well-connected to areas of population growth. Moreover, industrial and commercial developments have continued to contribute to sprawl. And so, while the government established a new form of comprehensive integrated plan that would link housing, urban planning and transportation more effectively, plan coverage was proceeding slowly and leapfrog developments continued apace.

In 2010, the "15 km" rule was extended to cover more municipalities. In 2013, it was expanded again to apply to municipalities around cities of 15 000 and by 2017, all municipalities will be required to be covered by a SCoT, and if they are not, no new developments will be permitted in that locale. Thus, by 2017, all of France will be covered by the limited urbanisation principle.

Source: Ministère du Logement et de l'Égalité des territoires (2014), "Renforcement du principe d'urbanisation limitée en l'absence de SCoT", www.logement.gouv.fr/IMG/pdf/fiche_alur__absence_de_scot-principe_d_urbanisation_limitee.pdf.

Parallel planning systems

The preceding section has described the multi-scaled system of planning that exists in Poland. But it is important to recognise that there are parallel systems that operate outside of these logics. First, "special infrastructural acts", which in effect suspend common spatial law, have been successfully used to streamline major new public investments. But they have also been used to reduce public and municipal engagement and can lead to developments that contradict the local spatial plans. This may accelerate the execution of some projects; however, it creates a major problem as there is no cross-level co-ordination mechanism for such special investment (OECD, 2013a: 266).

Second, the mechanism for planning decisions grants approval for individual developments with little ability to shape their form or location. These developments may contradict the overarching spatial objectives of the municipality – such as the desire for a compact urban form. The allowance of new developments based on the characteristics of the neighbouring environ (where proximity is not clearly defined), can reproduce unwanted features as opposed to directing desirable uses. Beyond this, there is evidence that the planning decision mechanism is cumbersome and lengthens the time it takes to obtain building permits. A recent study found that in 84% of cases, planning decisions took two months or longer on average in 84% of cases (Polski Związek Firm Deweloperskich, 2015).

Third, the creation of special economic zones (SEZs) creates areas which are not linked into local spatial planning. These SEZs permit development in greenfield sites in advance of brownfield ones, which goes against the practices described in spatial planning strategies (national, local). In some instances these parallel systems may complement one another; however, in others, they are clearly working against one another. More should be done to reduce a reliance on extraordinary processes and incorporate these mechanisms into the planning system as a whole.

The planning system should be coherent as a whole. Presently these parallel structures create certain incentives which may be contrary to the aims of overarching strategies, potentially undermining their effectiveness.

Fiscal instruments to shape land use and development

While the use of regulatory instruments to shape land-use practices in Łódź is limited, so too are fiscal ones. The major fiscal instrument used by municipalities at present is the property tax, which is based on land and building size as opposed to its value. Consequently, when public investments – such as the major transportation and regeneration investments in the centre of Łódź – are developed, or land uses are changed (e.g. from agricultural to residential), the increase in value of impacted properties is not captured through the property tax. Moreover, the structure of the property tax may encourage land banking and speculation, which is contrary to the city's development objectives. At present, the property tax has limited effectiveness within the broader context of spatial planning objectives.

Property taxes are generally viewed as an efficient and equitable way of raising revenue. There are ongoing debates about whether an *ad valorum* tax on property should be adopted in Poland.[5] Such developments would need to carefully consider the tax base, the rate at which property would be taxed, how property would be assessed and how the tax would be collected. The OECD recommends that Poland adopt a full *ad valorum* (or cadastral) tax on property (OECD, 2008a; 2014). The rate should initially be set at a low level and should be accompanied by measures to ensure that low-income households can afford the tax without having to liquidate their property (OECD, 2008a: 16). There is a large amount of literature on the relative merits of different approaches which could inform such reforms (Slack and Bird, 2014; 2015).

It is worth noting that some researchers have expressed concerns regarding the quality of the cadastre system in Poland.[6] For example, Gluzak and Marona (2014) write that the "absence of [a] multipurpose cadastre system (indispensable for gathering, updating and disseminating real estate data) obstructs property tax administration and collection in Poland." The 2007 European Parliamentary Directive on Infrastructure for Spatial Information in the European Community (INSPIRE) has been adopted in Poland. The initiative seeks to make georeferenced data assessable, reliable, accurate and harmonised across datasets as much as possible. Poland is presently adopting new processes to meet the INSIPRE agenda which can support the adoption of *ad valorum* property taxation in the future.

Municipalities can also levy extraordinary fees to capture increases in land/property value as a result of public investments; however, there are limitations on their usage. Planning charges (or rents) and "adjacent/betterment" fees can be paid to a municipality where a property increases in value due to a change in land use, parcellation or new infrastructure. However, the charge cannot exceed 30%-50% of the value of the increase. In the case of planning charges, fees can only be levied if the owner has sold the property within a set number of years. In the case of adjacent fees, only adjacent (as the name suggests) properties are included. These mechanisms are limited, cumbersome and expensive to administer because of the need to value properties. It is likely for these reasons that such fees are not used in Łódź at present. The foregone revenue from increases in land value is potentially very large. For example, Polish municipalities converted 545 000 hectares of agricultural land to non-agricultural uses between 2004 and 2012 (Kowalewski et al., 2013). The increases in land value as a result of this conversion were generally not captured by fiscal instruments.

Łódź's spatial strategy describes a desire to see urban infilling and development of brownfield sites over that of greenfield ones but there are presently no tax-based or other fiscal incentives to encourage such uses. Brownfield sites can have complex ownership and be therefore more costly to develop than that of greenfield sites, which tend to be concentrated in ex/suburban areas. Similarly, smaller plots (infill sites) in the urban core may be less attractive for investors for this reason. A broader range of fiscal instruments could be employed to help meet these aims. While SEZs create a favourable regulatory and tax environment for private investment, they are not well integrated into broader spatial planning strategies and many of them encourage development on greenfield (as opposed to brownfield) sites.

Łódź is also undergoing a process of revitalisation in its urban core for which fiscal instruments could be employed – e.g. historical rehabilitation tax credits. Table 3.3 summarises a range of fiscal instruments that could be used by the city to shape development and better capture economic effects. The instruments that are presently being used are bolded. It should be noted that development impact fees presently have limited usage. Such fees are designed to transfer a portion of the capital cost from the public to the private investor. Further, it bears noting that the new Revitalisation Act creates the potential for two new fiscal tools: an adjacency levy and an expanded real estate tax.

Table 3.3. **Development management fiscal instruments**

Targeted fiscal instruments	Overarching fiscal instruments
Brownfield redevelopment incentives	Dedications (e.g. infrastructure levies)
Capital gains tax	**Development impact fees**[1]
Conservation easements	Land value tax
Historic rehabilitation tax credits	Linkage fees
Joint development	**Property tax**
Location efficient mortgages	Real estate transfer tax
Special economic zones	Special assessment tax
Split-property tax	Sub-division exactions
Tax increment financing	Tap fees
Transfer of development rights	
Use-value tax assessment	

Notes: Instruments that are presently being used are bolded. 1. These fees have limited usage at present.

Source: Modified from Silva, E.A. and R.A. Acheampong (2015), "Developing an inventory and typology of land-use planning systems and policy instruments in OECD countries", http://dx.doi.org/10.1787/5jrp6wgxp09s-en.

Functional urban areas: Linking rural and urban locales

There is little formal co-operation between urban and rural areas despite their close proximity and connections to one another. The regional authority may prepare the plans for the functional areas that act as supra-local planning documents, but they are not legally binding documents for local authorities. The latter, by constitutional law, have strong independence in terms of local planning. Municipalities co-ordinate on some issues – but as was described in the case of the rural commune of Nowosolna which borders Łódź's northeast – they are also in competition with one another for residents and businesses. There is a phenomenon of gentrification in many rural areas, such as those surrounding Łódź, which sets up rural municipalities to compete with the central city and also can lead to land use and other conflicts between residential suburbanising areas and industrial or agricultural land uses.

Further, inherent power asymmetries exist between large and small places. Interactions between rural and urban locales need to recognise and navigate these asymmetries related to resources, capacity and voice and carve out areas where they can meaningfully work with one another.[7] Commenting on this in an analysis of such partnerships in Łódź, Wójcik argues that "the basic condition for the creation of cohesion based on collaboration between local governments and local institutions is equality" (2014: 137). Partnerships are facilitated when the dominant city gives up some power to come to the table and act as an equal partner on issues, despite its greater resources, capacity and clout. Upper-level governments have a major role to play in structuring the incentives to do so. As OECD research has demonstrated, there are major benefits to overcoming metropolitan fragmentation (Ahrend et al., 2014).

The rural commune of Nowosolna is proactively working to address current and future land-use conflicts related to residential, agricultural and industrial uses. It is doing so by creating and consolidating separate zones for each type of activity through new land-use development plans. The commune is also developing its historical, cultural and natural assets to support tourism in the area and create a new central space – giving the commune a coherent identity which it now lacks. The areas of Łódź abutting Nowosolna fall under the city strategy's third zone (of housing and industrial estates, suburbs, non-urbanised areas) for which the major planning objective is to reduce urban sprawl. The city seeks to protect "spatial openness" by preventing the growth of single- and multi-family housing; prohibit the development of non-urbanised areas; and make sure that any new industrial or business investments are located in areas which are already well served by existing infrastructure (including telecommunications). Much development has already occurred in contradiction to these aims and the tools at the city's disposal to shape the desired compact urban form with distinct spaces are somewhat limited. Given this, there is residential growth in areas of Łódź abutting Nowosolna.

Nowosolna's desired spatial development is not necessarily in contradiction to that of Łódź's – taken together they describe a system with distinct land uses based on function. It is the nature of the connections between the two places and how those connections are governed which will matter to long-term outcomes. The viability of Nowosolna depends on its connections to Łódź, particularly transportation connections. The attractiveness of the area for residents is important to its development. Fragmented urban sprawl, mixed and conflicting land uses, and pressures on transportation, are detractions for both locales and hence offer an arena for co-operation. Upper-level governments have a role to play in creating incentives to facilitate this through governance structures and regulatory and fiscal instruments.

Presently, the EU integrated territorial investments (ITI) are creating such incentives. Metropolitan co-operation on projects is required in order to access ITI funds. In Łódź, a metropolitan area association has been created to this end (established April 2014). At present, the association includes Łódź and cities and townships in four counties: Pabianice, Eastern Łódź, Brzeziny and Zgierz. A first goal of the association is to develop a development strategy for the metropolitan area. The voluntary nature of this association leads to collaboration on projects that are mutually beneficial. This leads to the risk that important issues where municipal interests do not align with one another may not be undertaken. It is also the case that some projects, such as metropolitan transportation planning, may in fact incentivise sprawl by opening up new areas for investment, which is contrary to overarching spatial goals.

ITI EU funding requirements stipulate that two documents are required in order to apply for funds – a strategic diagnosis of the issues facing the area and a joint development strategy. Previous OECD research on rural-urban partnerships in the West Pomeranian region of Poland points to the importance of getting the geography right (OECD, 2013c). For partnerships to support more coherent spatial and land-use planning, the question of geography is paramount.

While EU funding has structured incentives for co-operation at present, this may change when funding inevitably declines. Commenting on Łódź's new form of association, Wójcik (2014) notes that:

> …the integration of local government entities around specific tasks should not only lead to the completion of predetermined investment tasks, but should also strengthen the Association in its pursuit of a higher system of planning and governance in the Łódź Metropolitan Area. However, actions of this type will need approval at higher levels of government; hence, the need for a national metropolitan area law. If this does not happen, then the proposed projects will come to a quick end and reduced financing from the European Union (after 2020) may cause a marked decline in the pursuit of cohesion, especially in the realm of functional integration. (2014: 136).

The national government has met this need for increased intermunicipal collaboration through the new Metropolitan Association Act (2015). This is an explicit form of partnership where there are common objectives, but no delegated functions (see Box 3.4 for further discussion on rural-urban governance frameworks).

Strengthening public engagement

Łódź has a growing culture of public engagement, including a thriving non-governmental sector that shows real interest in being a partner in planning and deliberative processes. At its core, public engagement is about involving "the public" (this can be any individual, group of individuals, organisation or institution that has an interest in or is affected by a decision) in the policy process. There is growing recognition that public engagement is an essential component of good governance; that it is an important foundation for openness, accountability and transparency. By gathering multiple viewpoints on an issue and creating a space for open deliberation, public engagement efforts are meant to lead to more intelligent policy making by taking a range of views, needs, information and interests into account. This can result in more effective outcomes by negotiating trade-offs and building consensus on issues upfront, before they descend into conflict, including recourse to litigation.

In Łódź, a variety of public engagement efforts on planning issues were described; some were structured to meaningfully engage citizens in decision-making processes on issues that affected them (with reported positive outcomes), while others entailed a minimum of consultation and received poor attendance and low engagement as a result. It was also reported that in some instances there has been low buy-in from municipal politicians for public engagement efforts and that, in general, there are low levels of social trust. This is not a particular reflection of Łódź – rather it is a reflection of broader national historical legacies in Poland where social trust is relatively low (Lasinka, 2013; OECD, 2008a: 172).

Box 3.4. Governance frameworks for rural-urban partnerships

A recent study on rural-urban partnerships conducted by the OECD revealed some common elements. In case studies of 11 rural-urban partnerships in a range of OECD countries, 4 different ways to approach rural-urban collaborations emerge. Each reflects the specific institutional and cultural context of the country. This framework divides the partnerships observed into an admittedly simplified schema, to tease out key aspects that can guide policy development and support (see Figure 3.1 for a summary).

Figure 3.1. **Types of rural-urban partnerships**

Explicit rural-urban partnership	Implicit urban-rural partnership
• Rennes (France) • Geelong (Australia) • Nuremberg (Germany) • Central Zone of West Pomeranian Voivodeship (Poland • BrabantStad (Netherlands)	• Forlì-Cesena (Italy) • Extremadura (Spain) • Castelo Branco (Portugal) • Central Finland (Jyväskylä and Saarijärvi-Viitasaari) (Finland) • Lexington (United States) • Prague/Central Bohemia (Czech Republic)

Model 1	Model 2	Model 3	Model 4
Delegated functions	**No delegated functions**	**Delegated functions**	**No delegated functions**
• Rennes (France)	• Geelong (Australia) • Nuremberg (Germany) • Central Zone of West Pomeranian Voivodeship (Poland) • BrabantStad (Netherlands)	• Extremadura (Spain) • Forlì-Cesena (Italy)	• Lexington (United States) • Prague (Czech Republic) • Central Finland (Jyväskylä and Saarijärvi-Viitasaari) (Finland) • Castelo Branco (Portugal)

The categories "explicit" and "implicit" are used to highlight an important distinction between the 11 rural-urban partnerships analysed. The "explicit" rural-urban partnerships (five in total), deliberately set out to cultivate a rural-urban partnership or manage rural-urban relationships. This "intent" is reflected in the objectives of the partnership agreement. This rural-urban dimension is a core aspect for the partnership that is deliberately pursued, either through the issues identified, initiatives realised and/or stakeholder involvement.

In contrast, the "implicit" group (six cases) shows no such overt objective. In these cases, the collaboration that emerged was driven by other local development objectives mandating the involvement of urban and rural areas. The second layer sub-divides the two groups further, based on the partnerships' delegated authority. Delegation of authority means division of authority and powers downwards. This means the partnerships have some semblance of recognition, such that they have been entrusted with the responsibility to act. This provides clues to the level or recognition (by other levels of government), its ability to realise objectives (implementation tools) and financial acumen.

Each type presents various advantages and disadvantages. On the topic of spatial planning, the case of Rennes, France offers a unique approach – it is an inter-municipal structure called Rennes Métropole with a dedicated revenue source that elaborates a common spatial plan for the territory that is then binding for local land-use plans. The Territorial Coherence Plan (*Schéma de cohérence territoriale*, or SCoT) allows Rennes Métropole to directly manage rural and urban issues and present a unified voice on behalf of the region. It is able to effectively incorporate and then work with smaller peri-rural municipalities towards the realisation of an overall vision for Rennes. The partnership is also able to take advantage of its large organisational structure and stakeholders. Nonetheless, there can be some drawbacks, such as less local autonomy – municipalities agree upon joining to cede certain powers, which they are no longer authorised to exercise.

Source: OECD (2013c), *Rural-Urban Partnerships: An Integrated Approach to Economic Development*, http://dx.doi.org/10.1787/9789264204812-en.

The effective engagement of citizens in decision making requires the devolution of power to a certain extent and it is important senior administrators and municipal politicians take part in and are accountable to the process. It is also important that such activities are well-structured and consistent; that individuals are involved early in the process; that they have the information needed to be effective in their engagement; and that the outcomes of such activities are reported. The system of planning by decision makes it difficult for citizens to understand the direction of development in the city. In effect, the randomness of one-off decisions undermines land-use planning and the city's vision for sustainable urban development. This mechanism should be reduced or eliminated.

There are many things that a city can do to make developments in the city more understandable to citizens and easier to engage in. For example, in France, all planning documents have been digitised (Box 3.5) and a website lets residents easily visualise the plans that are relevant to them. A centre of expertise on public engagement can be very instrumental in ensuring that public engagement efforts are effective and co-ordinated and would be an important step in increasing what have traditionally been low levels of engagement in the city.

Box 3.5. The digitisation of planning documents: Example of France

It is often remarked that citizen engagement remains low for land-use planning issues due to a lack of information (Purian, Ahituv and Ashkenazy, 2012). To this end, France has embarked on a process of digitisation for planning documents in order to reduce costs and improve communication between those involved in the process. In this way, planning documents are easily shared, updated and made accessible for elected officials, professions and stakeholders. The new process is expected to be cheaper, editable, exchangeable and multipliable. Presently, urban planning documents can be scanned at an estimated cost of EUR 500 while an individual hard copy can cost EUR 100. Significant costs savings are expected, particularly when one factors in that fact that it is much easier to make revisions to scanned versions.

- Communes must make their planning documents accessible online by 1 January 2016.
- Between 1 January 2016 and 1 January 2020, when communes develop or revise a planning document, they need to scan the national format (Conseil national de l'information géographique).
- From 1 January 2020, authorities must publish their planning documents on the Geoportal of urban planning to make them enforceable. The site, currently being established, will be the national portal to all of the urban information in France.

This process of digitisation makes information incredibly fast and easy to access. For example, from a city's online land-use plan it is possible to research information relevant to any parcel of land either by using its cadastral reference, civic address or simply by zoning in on the map. The relevant plans and regulations pertaining to the parcel of land selected are automatically pulled up. Further map layers can be added to see the location of major risks (e.g. transportation of dangerous materials), mobile towers, hydroelectric studies, sports centres, and health services and multimodal transportation routes.

The digitisation of planning documents meets the European Directive INSPIRE to provide citizens with geotagged information on sustainable development issues (Ordinance No. 2013-1184 of 19 December 2013).

Source: Government of France (2015), Ministry of Housing, Territorial Equality and Rural Policy. www.territoires.gouv.fr/la-numerisation-des-documents-d-urbanisme.

The city's revitalisation process, together with its overarching goals to create a denser and more liveable urban core, demands effective public engagement with residents. The process of adopting local spatial development plans for the revitalisation area was a first step in this regard, but as further investments are made, city officials together with the revitalisation management committee, developers and residents will undoubtedly face further negotiations.

It is important to recognise that not all stakeholders come to the table with the same resources and knowledge. There is a large amount of literature on how to design participatory processes for individuals who are normally excluded from decision making by institutionalised inequalities (Bryson et al., 2013). Such engagement efforts may require stronger investments in time and resources from municipal officials and intermediary groups such as non-profit organisations and neighbourhood associations. The purpose and goals of such engagement efforts should be made clear upfront in order to set expectations. There are many reasons to put in the effort to design inclusive engagement strategies: they can lead to better urban design and planning, more inclusive neighbourhoods, and mediate any potential conflicts upfront. The redevelopment of Łódź's centre is taking place in an area of social deprivation. Inclusive engagement practices will be very important for this redevelopment as individuals will be rehoused in many circumstances as buildings are upgraded.

The use of public-private partnerships for developments can sometimes present an obstacle to the public engagement process. For example, confidentiality clauses in public-private partnerships can limit meaningful public participation. Some best practices to get around this problem include:

> …1) using a clear and narrow standard for what information should be kept confidential; 2) ensuring that public officials with responsibility for project decisions and their staffs have full access to all project information, including that not made public; 3) appointing a watchdog to see that these standards are upheld; and 4) implementing a decision process that allows public input and places the burden for proving that information should remain confidential on the entity making the request. (Siemiatycki, 2007: 388)

An even greater concern regarding the use of public-private partnerships is where the long-term consequences and cost to the public of the project are not clear – sometimes the financial implications can stretch over decades (Haylla and Wettenhall, 2010). Where public-private partnerships are employed, the city should take great care to ensure that risk is equally shared between the public and private actors and that the fiscal implications are evident to residents. In cases where a public space is highly controversial, unsolicited bids are involved, the procurement method is sole-sourced or councillors are funded by the private partner involved in the bid, the use of public-private partnerships should be reconsidered (Krawchenko and Stoney, 2011).

Meeting the challenge of deconcentration and depopulation

While Łódź experienced rapid growth during the industrial era, the population of the city and metropolitan area is presently shrinking and expected to continue to do so over the foreseeable future. Łódź joins the ranks of many cities worldwide that are experiencing the same phenomenon – over the past 50 years, 370 cities with populations over 100 000 have shrunk by at least 10% (Oswalt and Rieniets, 2007).

Cities have long been synonymous with growth and many planning instruments and fiscal tools are based on that logic. Population shrinkage – as it has come to be known – challenges planners and policy makers to operate in a vastly different environment, one where there will likely be much weaker housing demand, an abundance of vacant land and potentially, vacant buildings as well. There is a breadth of literature that explores these issues and offers tools and practices for cities experiencing population decline (Janssen-Jansen, 2015). There are innovative examples of how to address population decline in spatial planning from other post-socialist cities such as Leipzig and Dresden (Haase, 2008; Rink et al., 2012; Weichmann, 2008). Such cities bear a particular hallmark of large-scale housing settlements from the late 1960s and 1970s, which pose their own unique challenges.

In tandem to the trends of depopulation, Łódź has also an urban form that is deconcentrated – or sprawling. In particular, there is peri-urban growth in rural communes such as Nowosolna (Brzeziński, 2010). Low-density sprawling developments make it very difficult for municipalities to provide citizens with services and infrastructure. Services will tend to be at a greater distance from individuals and infrastructure becomes much more expensive to build, service and maintain. It is very difficult to provide public transportation in such environments, and consequently, there is a strong reliance on cars. An estimated 100 000 people travel into Łódź from the surrounding commuting zones on a daily basis.

Taken together, these two trends lead to the inefficient and potentially unsustainable allocation of public investments and land uses where there are fixed demands on infrastructure and fewer resources to pay for them. Maintenance of infrastructure and services may become "locked in" as individuals expect the same levels as they have experienced in the past. A deconcentrated urban form can make it much more difficult to maintain this.

Recognising these trends, Łódź is seeking a denser urban form, which is an important strategy for shrinking cities. Increasing urban density can significantly reduce energy consumption in urban areas, help preserve open green space and protect urban areas (OECD, 2011: 91). In Łódź, this densification comes in tandem with a massive regeneration effort which has the potential to price lower income residents out of the central areas. With a growing elder population, mobility and access to services becomes increasingly important.

The continued decline of population within the urban core of Łódź in combination with an increase in the population of suburban communities also makes it more difficult to provide efficient and cost-effective public transport. This is especially the case because population growth in suburban municipalities does not occur around transport hubs, but is spread out in low densities over large areas.

Consequently, sprawling suburban development threatens to increase car reliance in the long term. This has undesirable consequences for several reasons. First, it increases carbon emissions and air pollution, thereby contributing to climate change and harming the health of local residents. Second, it increases congestion, which reduces the productivity of the economy in the urban area due to the increased time it takes to move goods and people from one place to another. Third, increased car reliance harms the economic viability of the city centre, which is more difficult to reach by car than the urban periphery. Thus, it may counteract the desired rehabilitation of the city centre by reducing its attractiveness as a retail location and as a work place. Łódź's densification strategy is important because of the associated environmental and economic benefits.

Higher densities also increase productivity and consequently, GDP levels of an urban area. Generally, larger and denser cities have higher productivity levels than less populous and deconcentrated ones. While many factors are responsible for this phenomenon, an important explanation is so-called agglomeration economies. The term describes a number of effects that increase the productivity of firms and workers that operate in densely populated areas, for example because density fosters the spread of innovative ideas and business processes. It can be of important magnitude; a doubling of the population of a given area increases the productivity of its businesses by up to 5% (OECD, 2015b). Thus, Łódź's strategy to increase the density of its urban core is likely to reap benefits in the form of improved economic performance.

Positively, both city strategy documents and national legislation such as the Revitalisation Act (2015) emphasise the importance of social considerations alongside physical investments. These dynamic and evolving issues will require close monitoring. More refined and timely data at a smaller scale would help officials obtain a better understanding of changing conditions in order to react accordingly. This, combined with a broader range of planning tools and collaborative approaches, effective fiscal forecasting, and meaningful public engagement efforts will help city officials effectively adjust to changing conditions in an integrated manner.

Box 3.6. Embracing experimentation through temporary land uses

Vacant land – a feature common in cities facing depopulation – can pose a real problem. Overgrown and unsightly vacant properties detract from a city's livability and negatively affect real-estate prices. This can create dead zones in a community and reinforce the feeling of neighbourhood neglect and decline.

In response to this problem, urban activists have been transforming such spaces for decades, often without the permission of local authorities. These types of unsanctioned activities are sometimes referred to as "guerilla urbanism" – for example, the Green Guerilla movement in New York City which pioneered the practice of reclaiming vacant urban land for neighbourhood gardening in the 1970s (Schmelzkopf, 1995).

In many cases, these activist-driven movements have led to institutionalised practices. Community garden programmes supported by local government are now commonplace on vacant lots. Or, take for example, Park(ing) Day in San Francisco – an initiative started by a local activist group in 2005 which temporarily reclaimed parking spaces for pedestrian activities. Embracing the concept, the city has created a "Pavement to Parks" programme led by private initiative which has created dozens such temporary public spaces. "Do-It-Yourself" skateboard parks offer another example. The former Director of Design for the city of London describes the growth of temporary land-use initiatives as a "confluence of tough economic times, the emergence of a new kind of creative culture, and a preponderance of stalled development and vacant properties" (Greco, 2012).

Local governments are increasingly embracing the temporary land uses movement and working with communities and businesses to make better use of vacant spaces – whether this be for a pop-up event or festival or longer term uses that entail the refurbishment of built structures on vacant land. The approach has been referred to as the "temporary city", "tactical urbanism" or even the "pop-up city" – it is grounded in the idea that planning of public spaces doesn't always need to involve capital-intensive projects. The term "temporary" can entail anything from a couple of days to several years.

Box 3.6. **Embracing experimentation through temporary land uses** (*continued*)

A city's regulatory environment plays a major role in shaping the prospects for temporary land uses. For instance, Portland's open rules towards food vending have allowed local food truck entrepreneurs to occupy vacant spaces and create vibrant uses out of them – it has been a boon for local businesses and has encouraged tourism to the area (Southworth, 2014). Temporary land uses encourage experimentation. Across the United States, local skateboarders have taken over vacant lands – often unused public land underneath bridges – to build illegal skateparks (e.g. Burnside Park, Portland; Washington Street Park, San Diego). In many cases these illegal structures have since gained community buy-in and have been turned into official skateparks sanctioned by municipalities, thus changing their temporary land uses into permanent features of the urban landscape. Though initially an unsanctioned experiment, their uses were proven to be beneficial and were eventually accepted.

In Cleveland – a shrinking city where approximately 1 000 homes are demolished in a typical year – the need to address vacant land uses is paramount. The city, together with the Kent State University Urban Design Collaborative, created a "Vacant land re-use pattern book" (2009) as a guide and resource for individuals and communities wishing to undertake projects on vacant land. It provides cost estimates for different kinds of projects and access to data and maps of vacant land so that potential areas can be identified and linked up to other vacant sites. In an assessment of such practices, Németh and Langhorst (2013) offer some conditions for appropriate temporary uses (Table 3.4).

Table 3.4. **Conditions for appropriate temporary uses**

General category	More appropriate for temporary uses	Less appropriate for temporary uses
Ownership of the land	– Lack of (or poor efficacy of) public investment or incentives	– Private ownership (unless vacant too long)
Role/influence of the city	– Slow-growth/declining cities – Trial and error, flexible approach embraced – Socially progressive goals (inclusion, diversity, access)	– Traditional planning tools successfully encouraging private investment – Growing/vibrant cities – Top-down, master planning – Pragmatic, financial/economic goals only
General economic climate	– Low private development interest – Times of "disruptive, stressful, social and urban change" – Exploit uncertain transitional period	– High private development interest – More stable, predictable times – Imminent redevelopment likely
Development potential of the space	– Long-vacant land or structures – Vacant land/abandoned structures – Areas with high risk of decline and "contagion effect" – Non-corporate, low-capital businesses or investors likely – Smaller scale – Leftover/remnant parcels, small, fragmented spaces – Higher use value – Areas seeking redevelopment, attraction of new residents and businesses – Active community/residents/non-profits/small investors	– Recent vacancy; likely to redevelop quickly – "Underutilised land" (awaiting planned development) – Areas of stability – Corporate developers, big business, municipal "growth regimes" – Larger scale – Larger, continuous spaces – Higher exchange value – High-profile, central tourist areas – Top-down corporate interests
Potential uses of the space	– Events/programmatic uses – "Soft content" – Desire/need to break from mono-functional environments – Desire to encourage/create new meanings, functions, identities and relationships for/of a space – Test unfamiliar or potentially controversial ideas – Educational tool to prove investment potential of certain uses/spaces – "Tactical" unsanctioned and transgressive uses, frequently by marginalised demographics, subcultures (e.g. squatting, skateboarding, emergent artists...) (De Certeau, 1984)	– Fixed infrastructure, buildings – Inflexible built form – Already diverse, multi-use environments – More stable, secure areas – "Proven" solutions, uses – "Strategic" sanctioned uses catering to preferred/privileged/mainstream demographics (De Certeau, 1984)

Source: Németh, J. and J. Langhorst (2014), "Rethinking urban transformation: Temporary uses for vacant land", http://dx.doi.org/10.1016/j.cities.2013.04.007.

Box 3.6. **Embracing experimentation through temporary land uses** (*continued*)

As Németh and Langhorst (2013) note, there are liability issues to consider and not all temporary land uses will be desirable or feasible. Much depends on the compatibility of the uses with that of the surrounding neighbourhood, the type of ownership of the land, the built structures on it and liabilities associated with the activities that are planned. Nevertheless, by encouraging temporary land uses on vacant land – and creating guidelines and criteria for such uses – cities can work with communities and individuals to gauge what works, how land uses may evolve and create dynamic spaces that may either go on to last in the longer term or shift to new uses over time.

Sources: Greco, J. (2012). "From pop-up to permanent", www.des.ucdavis.edu/faculty/handy/ESP171/Pop-up.pdf; Németh, J. and J. Langhorst (2014). "Rethinking urban transformation: Temporary uses for vacant land", http://dx.doi.org/10.1016/j.cities.2013.04.007; Schmelzkopf, K. (1995), "Urban community gardens as contested space", http://dx.doi.org/10.2307/215279; Southworth, M. (2014), "Public life, public space, and the changing art of city design", http://dx.doi.org/10.1080/13574809.2014.854684.

Notes

1. Approved by the Resolution of the Council of Ministers on 20 October 2015.

2. For example, in a 2012 survey of municipalities and communes from the Krakow metropolitan area (excluding the city of Krakow), 51% rated the spatial planning and development system as "very poor" or "poor" (Hołuj and Zawilińska, 2013).

3. For example, a study by Tönkő and Kronenberg of Łódź's urban green infrastructure and planning governance found that while the Municipal Management and Environmental Protection Policy of the city sets many specific objectives and targets, it lacks proper monitoring mechanisms for urban green infrastructure (2015: 11). The study found that factors that enhance the implementation of the city's objective in this area include citizen advocacy, funding for investments in urban green spaces and municipal obligations defined in the sectoral policies accompanying the city's integrated development strategy (Tönkő and Kronenberg, 2015: 11). In contrast, factors that hinder the implementation of green infrastructure objectives were identified as special interests of individuals or groups (particularly developers), a lack of funding for such initiatives and poor co-operation among different units/departments within the municipality (Tönkő and Kronenberg, 2015: 11).

4. As of 2012, binding local land-use plans covered only 28% of land (OECD, 2015a: 11).

5. This is often referred to as a "cadastral" tax because it would be linked to such a national property register.

6. A cadastre is a comprehensive register of real estate or meters and bounds in a country; it is used to define the dimension and location of land parcels and typically contains information on land type, ownership and tenure. Poland has multiple cadastres based on land/resource type – e.g. real estate, forest, water, roads, farm.

These cadastres are maintained by different entities/ministries and as a result may contain duplication between them.

7. For example, this has been assessed as a major barrier to co-operation in the case of the Gdańsk metropolitan area (Czepczynski, 2009: 255).

Bibliography

Act on Special Economic Zones of 20 October 1994, Journal of Laws of 2007, No. 42, item 274, Journal of Laws of 2008, No. 118, item 746.

Ahrend, R. et al. (2014), "What makes cities more productive? Evidence on the role of urban governance from five OECD countries", *OECD Regional Development Working Papers*, No. 2014/05, OECD Publishing, Paris, http://dx.doi.org/10.1787/5jz432cf2d8p-en.

Assif, S. (2007), "Principles of Israel's Comprehensive National Outline Plan for Construction, Development and Conservation (NOP 35)", www.moin.gov.il/SubjectDocuments/Tma35_PrinciplesDocument.pdf.

Bryson, J. et al. (2013), "Designing public participation processes", *Public Administration Review*, Vol. 73/1, pp. 23-34, http://dx.doi.org/10.1111/j.1540-6210.2012.02678.x.

Brzeziński, C. (2010), Procesy suburbanizacji obszarów podmiejskich na przykładzie gmin powiatu pabianickiego, *Zmiany przestrzenne*.

City of Łódź (2012), Integrated Development Strategy for Lodz 2020+, Resolution No. XLIII/824/12 of the City Council in Łódź of 25 June 2012, http://bip.uml.lodz.pl/_plik.php?id=35030 (accessed 25 March 2016).

Cleveland Urban Design Collaborative (2009), "Reimagining Cleveland vacant land reuse pattern book", Kent State University, Cleveland, Ohio, www.scribd.com/doc/61854154/ReImagining-Cleveland-Pattern-Book (accessed 25 March 2016).

Czepczynski, M. (2009), "Regionalisation in the Gdańsk area: Virtual disintegration and functional cooperation", *International Journal of Public Sector Management*, Vol. 22/3, pp. 249-259, http://dx.doi.org/10.1108/09513550910949226.

De Certeau (1984), *Walking in the city*, University of California Press.

Gluszak, M. and B. Marona (2014), "Property tax and the fiscal independence of Polish local government", *Актуальні проблеми економіки*, Vol. 6, pp. 364-373, http://irbis-nbuv.gov.ua/cgi-bin/irbis_nbuv/cgiirbis_64.exe?C21COM=2&I21DBN=UJRN&P21DBN=UJRN&IMAGE_FILE_DOWNLOAD=1&Image_file_name=PDF/ape_2014_6_45.pdf.

Government of France (2015), Ministry of Housing, Territorial Equality and Rural Policy, www.territoires.gouv.fr/la-numerisation-des-documents-d-urbanisme (accessed 25 March 2016).

Government of Israel (2015), "Integrated planning in Israel", www.moin.gov.il/Subjects/GeneralPlaning/Pages/default.aspx (accessed 25 March 2016).

Government of Poland (2012), "Summary of the National Spatial Development Concept 2030", Ministry of Regional Development.

Government of Poland (2007), Report of the Polish Ministry of Infrastructure, http://warszawa.sarp.org.pl/pliki/raportMBud2007_04.pdf?PHPSESSID=47f2e722vtlkncjln8p3bhp0m1 (accessed 25 March 2016).

Greco, J. (2012), "From pop-up to permanent", *Planning*, Vol. 78/9, pp. 15-18, www.des.ucdavis.edu/faculty/handy/ESP171/Pop-up.pdf.

Haase, D. (2008), "Urban ecology of shrinking cities: An unrecognized opportunity?", *Nature and Culture*, Vol. 3/1, pp. 1-8, http://dx.doi.org/10.3167/nc.2008.030101.

Havel, M.B. (2014), "Delineation of property rights as institutional foundations for urban land markets in transition", *Land Use Policy*, Vol. 38, pp. 615-626, http://dx.doi.org/10.1016/j.landusepol.2014.01.004.

Hayllar, M.R. and R. Wettenhall (2010), "Public-private partnerships: Promises, politics and pitfalls", *Australian Journal of Public Administration*, Vol. 69/S1, pp. 1-7, http://dx.doi.org/10.1111/j.1467-8500.2009.00657.x.

Healey, P. (2006), "Territory, integration and spatial planning", in: Tewdwr-Jones, M. and P. Allmendinger (eds.), *Territory, Identity and Spatial Planning: Spatial Governance in a Fragmented Nation*, Routledge, pp. 64-79.

Holuj, A. and B. Zawilińska (2013), "Planning documents issued in Poland at the municipal level: Example of the Krakow metropolitan area", *Journal of Settlements and Spatial Planning*, Vol. 4/1, pp. 125, http://geografie.ubbcluj.ro/ccau/jssp/arhiva_1_2013/14JSSP012013.pdf.

Janssen-Jansen, L. (2015), "Part I planning challenges in a context of discontinuous growth", in: Leshinsky, R. and C. Legacy (eds.), *Instruments of Planning: Tensions and Challenges for More Equitable and Sustainable Cities*, Routledge, pp. 11-19.

Kowalewski, A. et al. (2013), "Raport o ekonomicznych stratach i społecznych kosztach niekontrolowanej suburbanizacji w Polsce", Fundacja Rozwoju Demokracji Lokalnej, IGiPZ PAN, Warsaw.

Krawchenko, T. and C. Stoney (2011), "Public private partnerships and the public interest: A case study of Ottawa's Lansdowne Park development", *Canadian Journal of Nonprofit and Social Economy Research*, Vol. 2/2, pp. 74-90, http://anserj.ca/index.php/cjnser/article/view/92.

Lasinska, K. (2013), *Social Capital in Eastern Europe: Poland an Exception?*, Springer Science and Business Media.

Mackowiak-Pandera, J. and B. Jessel (2006), "Developments of SEA in Poland", in: Schmidt, M., E. Joao and E. Albrecht (eds.), *Implementing Strategic Environmental Assessment*, Springer Science and Business Media.

Miasta Łodzi (2015), Raport z konsultacji społecznych projektu budżetu miasta Łodzi na 2016 rok oraz projektu Wieloletniej Prognozy Finansowej miasta Łodzi na lata 2016-2040, http://bip.uml.lodz.pl/_plik.php?id=43359 (accessed 25 March 2016).

Ministère du Logement et de l'Égalité des territoires (2014), "Renforcement du principe d'urbanisation limitée en l'absence de SCoT", Loi pour l'accès au logement et un urbanisme rénové No. 2014-366 du 24 mars 2014, www.logement.gouv.fr/IMG/pdf/fiche_alur_absence_de_scot-principe_d_urbanisation_limitee.pdf.

Najwyższa Izba Kontroli (2013), Lokalizacja inwestycji na obszarach objętych ochroną przyrody w województwie Podlaskim, Informacja o wynikach kontroli, www.nik.gov.pl/plik/id,7229,vp,9113.pdf.

Németh, J. and J. Langhorst (2014). "Rethinking urban transformation: Temporary uses for vacant land", *Cities*, Vol. 40, pp. 143-150, http://dx.doi.org/10.1016/j.cities.2013.04.007.

New Centre of Łódź (2015), "Revitalization of the centre of Łódź".

OECD (2016), *OECD Territorial Reviews: Japan 2016*, OECD Publishing, Paris, http://dx.doi.org/10.1787/9789264250543-en.

OECD (2015a), *OECD Environmental Performance Reviews: Poland 2015*, OECD Publishing, Paris, http://dx.doi.org/10.1787/9789264227385-en.

OECD (2015b), *The Metropolitan Century: Understanding Urbanisation and its Consequences*, OECD Publishing, Paris, http://dx.doi.org/10.1787/9789264228733-en.

OECD (2014), *OECD Economic Surveys: Poland 2014*, OECD Publishing, Paris, http://dx.doi.org/10.1787/eco_surveys-pol-2014-en.

OECD (2013a), *Poland: Implementing Strategic-State Capability*, OECD Public Governance Reviews, OECD Publishing, Paris, http://dx.doi.org/10.1787/9789264201811-en.

OECD (2013b), *OECD Regions at a Glance 2013*, OECD Publishing, Paris, http://dx.doi.org/10.1787/reg_glance-2013-en.

OECD (2013c), *Rural-Urban Partnerships: An Integrated Approach to Economic Development*, OECD Publishing, Paris, http://dx.doi.org/10.1787/9789264204812-en.

OECD (2012), *Compact City Policies: A Comparative Assessment*, OECD Green Growth Studies, OECD Publishing, Paris, http://dx.doi.org/10.1787/9789264167865-en.

OECD (2011), *OECD Urban Policy Reviews, Poland 2011*, OECD Publishing, Paris, http://dx.doi.org/10.1787/9789264097834-en.

OECD (2008b), *OECD Economic Surveys: Poland 2008*, OECD Publishing, Paris, http://dx.doi.org/10.1787/eco_surveys-pol-2008-en.

OECD (2008a), *OECD Territorial Reviews: Poland 2008*, OECD Publishing, Paris, http://dx.doi.org/10.1787/9789264049529-en.

Oswalt, P. and T. Rieniets (2007), "Global context, shrinking cities", www.shrinkingcities.com/index.php?id=33&L=1 (accessed 25 March 2016).

Polski Związek Firm Deweloperskich (2015), Data, www.pzfd.pl (accessed 10 May 2016).

Purian, R., N. Ahituv and A. Ashkenazy (2012), "The richness of barriers to public participation: Multi-layered system of real estate data from multiple sources", *MCIS 2012 Proceedings*, Paper 17, http://aisel.aisnet.org/mcis2012/17.

Radzimski, A. (2012), "Real estate taxation in Poland and its influence on spatial development", in: Schrenk, M. et al. (eds.), *REAL CORP 2012: Remixing the City – Towards Sustainability and Resilience*.

Rink, D. et al. (2012), "From long-term shrinkage to re-growth? The urban development trajectories of Liverpool and Leipzig", *Built Environment*, Vol. 38/2, pp. 162-178, http://dx.doi.org/10.2148/benv.38.2.162.

Schmelzkopf, K. (1995). "Urban community gardens as contested space", *Geographical Review*, Vol. 1, pp. 364-381, http://dx.doi.org/10.2307/215279.

Siemiatycki, M. (2007), "What's the secret? Confidentiality in planning infrastructure using public/private partnerships", *Journal of the American Planning Association*, Vol. 73/4, pp. 388-403, http://dx.doi.org/10.1080/01944360708978520.

Silva, E.A. and R.A. Acheampong (2015), "Developing an inventory and typology of land-use planning systems and policy instruments in OECD countries", *OECD Environment Working Papers*, No. 94, OECD Publishing, Paris, http://dx.doi.org/10.1787/5jrp6wgxp09s-en.

Slack, E. and R.M. Bird (2015), "How to reform the property tax: Lessons from around the world", *IMFG Papers on Municipal Finance and Governance*, No. 21, http://munkschool.utoronto.ca/imfg/uploads/325/1689_imfg_no.21_online_final.pdf.

Slack, E. and R.M. Bird (2014), "The political economy of property tax reform", *OECD Working Papers on Fiscal Federalism*, No. 18, OECD Publishing, Paris, http://dx.doi.org/10.1787/5jz5pzvzv6r7-en.

Southworth, M. (2014). "Public life, public space, and the changing art of city design", *Journal of Urban Design*, Vol. 19/1, pp. 37, http://dx.doi.org/10.1080/13574809.2014.854684.

Statistical Office in Łódź (2014), *Statistics of Łódź 2014*, http://lodz.stat.gov.pl/en (accessed 25 March 2016).

Tönkő, A. and J. Kronenberg (2015), "Łódź, Poland: Case study city portrait; Part of a GREEN SURGE study on urban green infrastructure planning and governance in 20 European cities", Green Surge, Metropolitan Research Institute, Budapest, http://greensurge.eu/products/case-studies/Case_Study_Portrait_lodz.pdf.

Uchwała Nr 218/2008, Prezydium Państwowej Komisji Akredytacyjnej z dnia 10 kwietnia 2008 r, http://a.umed.pl/procesbolonski/materialy/PKA_kryteria_studenckie.pdf.

Weichmann, T. (2008), "Errors expected: Aligning urban strategy with demographic uncertainty in shrinking cities", *International Planning Studies*, Vol. 13/4, pp. 431-446, http://dx.doi.org/10.1080/13563470802519097.

Wójcik, M. (2014), "Rural-urban collaboration in a large metropolitan area: The Łódź metropolitan area case study", in: Dej, M., K. Janas and O. Wolski (eds.), *Towards Urban-Rural Partnerships in Poland: Preconditions and Potential*, Institute of Urban Development, Krakow, Poland, pp. 123-140.

Glossary

* Please note, the names of various plans and acts have been shorted in English usage in this report for the sake of simplicity.

Development Strategy for the Łódźkie Region 2020 (*Strategia Rozwoju Województwa Łódzkiego 2020*): Presents a regional analysis of spatial trends and regional visions and goals.

Integrated Development Strategy for Łódź 2020+ (*Strategia Zintegrowanego Rozwoju Łodzi 2020+*): Defines the long-term development objectives of the city and includes recommendations on economic, social and spatial development.

Local Spatial Development Plan (*Miejscowy plan zagospodarowania przestrzennego*): Determines local area spatial development including land-use provisions and building requirements (e.g. density and height requirements). Once adopted by a bylaw, these plans are legally binding. In other countries, these may be referred to as local spatial development plans. In other OECD countries, such plans are commonly referred to as land-use plans.

Metropolitan Association Act 2015 (*Ustawa o związkach metropolitalnych*): This recently adopted act outlines the conditions and requirements by which local governments may form a metropolitan association in order to address common issues, such as public transport.

National Spatial Development Concept 2030 (*Koncepcja Przestrzennego Zagospodarowania Kraju 2030*): Presents a vision of spatial development of Poland to 2030, defines goals and objectives of the national spatial development policy to facilitate its implementation, and provides for the rules and mechanisms for co-ordination and implementation of public development policies featuring a significant territorial impact.

Planning decisions (*Decyzje o warunkach zabudowy i zagospodarowania terenu*): The mechanisms used to grant permission for building construction or change of land use requests where an area is not covered by a valid local spatial development plan.

Regional Spatial Development Plan of (Łódzkie) Voivodeship (*Plan Zagospodarowania Przestrzennego Województwa Łódzkiego*): This plan presents a long-term perspective for the development of the region over the next 20 years. It defines the goals and directions of spatial development for the region. It includes arrangements concerning the location of supra-local investments and co-ordinates between national and local planning.

Spatial Development Strategy for Łódź 2020+ (*Strategia Przestrzennego Rozwoju Łodzi 2020+*): Defines the scope of the metropolitan area and makes recommendations on urban density. It is a sectoral policy following the Integrated Development Strategy for Łódź 2020+.

Spatial Planning and Development Act 2003 (*Ustawa o planowaniu i zagospodarowaniu przestrzennym*): Granted a decisive role to local governments for spatial and land-use planning.

Spatial study (*Studium uwarunkowań i kierunków zagospodarowania przestrzennego gminy*): Such "studies" are defined under the Spatial Planning and Development Act 2003. The elaboration and adoption of the "study" is compulsory for municipalities but as a document it is not binding on planning decisions. The full English translation of this type of plan is the "Study on the conditions and directions of spatial development".

Special infrastructural acts (*Specustawy inwestycyjne*): A series of acts to support the development of infrastructure or other assets that are deemed critical for national interest. These acts suspend local planning law.

ORGANISATION FOR ECONOMIC CO-OPERATION AND DEVELOPMENT

The OECD is a unique forum where governments work together to address the economic, social and environmental challenges of globalisation. The OECD is also at the forefront of efforts to understand and to help governments respond to new developments and concerns, such as corporate governance, the information economy and the challenges of an ageing population. The Organisation provides a setting where governments can compare policy experiences, seek answers to common problems, identify good practice and work to co-ordinate domestic and international policies.

The OECD member countries are: Australia, Austria, Belgium, Canada, Chile, the Czech Republic, Denmark, Estonia, Finland, France, Germany, Greece, Hungary, Iceland, Ireland, Israel, Italy, Japan, Korea, Latvia, Luxembourg, Mexico, the Netherlands, New Zealand, Norway, Poland, Portugal, the Slovak Republic, Slovenia, Spain, Sweden, Switzerland, Turkey, the United Kingdom and the United States. The European Union takes part in the work of the OECD.

OECD Publishing disseminates widely the results of the Organisation's statistics gathering and research on economic, social and environmental issues, as well as the conventions, guidelines and standards agreed by its members.

OECD PUBLISHING, 2, rue André-Pascal, 75775 PARIS CEDEX 16
(04 2016 08 1 P) ISBN 978-92-64-26053-5 – 2016

www.ingramcontent.com/pod-product-compliance
Lightning Source LLC
LaVergne TN
LVHW081410110826
845149LV00010B/1695

* 9 7 8 9 2 6 4 2 6 0 5 3 5 *